Crazy Quilts

1. Crazy quilt by Julia Chappell Skillman, Connecticut, 1886, 70″ × 66″. (Collection of Oregon Historical Society)

Crazy Quilts

Penny McMorris

E. P. DUTTON   NEW YORK

Detail from quilt by Julia Chappell Skillman, 1886, illustrated on page ii. (Collection of Oregon Historical Society)

Page i: Detail from quilt by Julia Chappell Skillman, 1886, illustrated on page ii. (Collection of Oregon Historical Society)

DUTTON STUDIO BOOKS/Published by the Penguin Group: Penguin Books USA Inc., 375 Hudson Street, New York, New York, 10014, U.S.A.; Penguin Books Ltd, 27 Wrights Lane, London W8 5TZ, England; Penguin Books Australia Ltd, Ringwood, Victoria, Australia; Penguin Books Canada Ltd, 2801 John Street, Markham, Ontario, Canada L3R 1B4; Penguin Books (N.Z.) Ltd, 182–190 Wairau Road, Auckland 10, New Zealand/ Penguin Books Ltd, Registered Offices: Harmondsworth, Middlesex, England./Published by Dutton Studio Books, an imprint of Penguin Books USA Inc./All rights reserved, 1984, under International and Pan-American Copyright Conventions./Library of Congress Catalog Card Number: 83-73452/Printed and bound by Dai Nippon Printing Co., Ltd., Tokyo, Japan./Without limiting the rights under copyright reserved above, no part of this publication may be reproduced, stored in or introduced into a retrieval system, or transmitted, in any form, or by any means (electronic, mechanical, photocopying, recording, or otherwise), without the prior written permission of both the copyright owner and the publisher of the book./ISBN: 0-525-48409-4.
10 9 8 7 6

Contents

Acknowledgments

It is a pleasure to give special thanks to Cuesta Benberry, Barbara Brackman, Ricky Clark, Sally Garoutte, and Joyce Gross for so generously sharing research material with me; to Buck McMorris for his patient help in searching for crazy quilts in England; to Charles and Cynthia Crow for manuscript suggestions; to my editor Cyril I. Nelson for his enthusiastic acceptance of the original idea for this book and for helpful suggestions about material and illustrations; to photographers Jim Birr, Tim Branco, Tom Burk, Lance Ferraro, George Freeman, John Glascock, Bill House, Frank Kiss, John Kluesener, and Schecter Me Sun Lee for their fine work; and to my daughters, Erin and Megan, for their understanding. Also, I am indebted to Virginia Clarke of Virginia Clarke Design, who did such a fine job of designing the book.

I also wish to express my gratitude to the following individuals and institutions for all the help and material received from them for the book.

Individuals: Gheen Abbott III, Patty Armstrong, Dorothy Beers, Elizabeth Birr, Dorothy Bond, Lillian Buckholts, Robert and Helen Cargo, Hazel Carter, Alta and Charles Codding, Carol Crabb, Addie Mangoian Davis, Gayle Fraas, Gordon and Ruth Donhouse, Helen Grigg, Chad Hagen, Joy Haley, Virginia Jacobs, Emily Johnson, Barbara and Clementine Kasselmann, Helen Kelly, Irma Koski, Dorothy S. Leighton, Rachel Maines, Richard Marquis, Mildred McKesson, Paul T. Millikin, Sandra Mitchell, Beth Mulholland, Jan Myers, Betsy Oliphant, Peggy Petrucci, Betty Peyton, Bets Ramsey, Nancy Ray, Robin Lehrer Roi, Bev Rush, Catherine Ryan, Mr. and Mrs. Robert Schneebeck, Sally Schreiber, Cathy Shoe, Duncan Slade, Merry Silber, Marcia and Ronald Spark, Nancy Starr, Pat Valerio, and Gail Winkler.

Institutions: Allen Memorial Art Museum, Oberlin, Ohio; Helen L. Allen Textile Collection, University of Wisconsin, Madison, Wisconsin; America Hurrah Antiques, New York City; Aspen Historical Society, Aspen, Colorado; Nancy J. Bromberg and Mary K. Popma, Turtle Creek Country Store, Chicago, Illinois; Center for the History of American Needlework, Ambridge, Pennsylvania; Connecticut Historical Society, Hartford, Connecticut; Cooper-Hewitt Museum, Smithsonian Institution, New York City; Kathy Dirks, National Museum of American History, Smithsonian Institution, Washington, D.C.; Amy Finkel, M. Finkel & Daughter, Philadelphia, Pennsylvania; Firelands Historical Society, Norwalk, Ohio; Greenfield Village and Henry Ford Museum, Dearborn, Michigan; Haggin Museum, Stockton, California; Indianapolis Museum of Art, Indianapolis, Indiana; Roderick Kiracofe and Michael Kile, San Francisco, California; Gracie Larsen, The Lace Museum, Mountain View, California; Lorain County Historical Society, Elyria, Ohio; Audrey G. Milne, York Institute Museum, Saco, Maine; Minnesota Historical Society, St. Paul, Minnesota; Missouri Historical Society, St. Louis, Missouri; Jeremy Farrell, Museum of Costume and Textiles, Nottingham, England; Museum of Our National Heritage, Lexington, Massachusetts; The Newark Museum, Newark, New Jersey; Oregon Historical Society, Portland, Oregon; *The Quilt Digest*, San Francisco, California; Linda Reuther and Julie Silber, Mary Strickler's Quilt; Elise Ronsheim, Ohio Historical Society, Columbus, Ohio; Seneca Falls Historical Society, Seneca Falls, New York; Carolyn Shine, Cincinnati Art Museum, Cincinnati, Ohio; State Historical Society of Wisconsin, Madison, Wisconsin; Jeanne H. Watson, Morris County Historical Society, Morristown, New Jersey; Welsh Folk Museum, St. Fagans, Cardiff, Wales; Thos. K. Woodard: American Antiques & Quilts, New York City; and Worthing Museum, Worthing, England.

The Crazy Quilt

Oh, say, can you see by the dawn's early light,
    What you failed to perceive at the twilight's last gleaming;
A crazy concern that through the long night
    O'er the bed where you slept was so saucily streaming;
        The silk patches so fair,
            Round, three-cornered and square
            Gives proof that the lunatic bed-quilt is there.
Oh, the crazy-quilt mania triumphantly raves,
And maid, wife and widow are bound as its slaves.

On that quilt dimly seen as you rouse from your sleep
    Your long-missing necktie in silence reposes,
And the filoselle insects that over it creep,
    A piece of your vest half-conceals, half discloses;
        There is Kensington-stitch
        In designs that are rich,
            Snow-flake, arrasene, point russe and all sich.
Oh, the crazy-quilt mania, how long will it rave?
And how long will fair woman be held as its slave?

And where is the wife who so vauntingly swore
    That nothing on earth her affections could smother?
She crept from your side at the chiming of four
    And is down in the parlor at work on another.
        Your breakfasts are spoiled,
        And your dinners half-boiled,
            And your efforts to get a square supper are foiled
By the crazy-quilt mania that fiendishly raves,
And to which all the women are absolute slaves.

And thus it has been since the panic began,
    In many loved homes it has wrought desolation,
And cursed is the power by many a man,
    That has brought him so close to the verge of starvation.
        But make it she must,
        She will do it or bust,
            Beg, swap, and buy pieces, or get them on trust.
Oh, the crazy-quilt mania, may it soon cease to rave
In the land of the free and the home of the brave.

—ANONYMOUS (reprinted from
Good Housekeeping,
October 25, 1890, p. 310)

2. Crazy quilt inscribed "Made by Grandma Hanshett for Lafayette, Anno Domini 1883." 59" × 47". Inasmuch as that great popular hero, the Marquis de Lafayette, died in 1834, one wonders what prompted the quiltmaker to dedicate her work to him so many years after his passing. Photograph courtesy America Hurrah Antiques, New York City. (Private collection)

Introduction

Never has there been such intense interest in a particular quilt style as there was in the crazy quilt during the period 1876–1900. The Singer Sewing Machine Company used the crazy quilt as a symbol on trade cards; women's periodicals gave directions for making crazy quilts and table covers, along with patterns for decorating them; silk manufacturers promoted the use of their scrap waste in making crazy quilts; cotton fabric was printed to resemble crazy quilts; short stories and poems were written about them; booklets on making crazy quilts were used as premiums in exchange for magazine subscriptions; and entire quilt shows were hung with crazy quilts (with the prizes from one show disappearing as quickly as the organizer—more about this later).

Definition

Many Victorian quilts made of fancy dress fabrics and embellished with areas of decorative embroidery are called *crazy quilts*. For the purpose of this book, however, a crazy quilt will be defined according to the definition found in *Webster's New World Dictionary of the American Language*, which limits the term *crazy quilt* to "a quilt made of pieces of cloth of various colors and irregular shapes and sizes."[1] This definition would include quilts made of cotton and wool, as well as silk. It would also include quilts with little or no embroidery. While not all of the quilts pictured in this book are typical crazy quilts, and some may seem to stretch the above definition a bit, all have at least some areas of the random, irregular patches so characteristic of crazy quilts.

Origin of Crazy Quilts

The crazy quilt has become known as the oldest American quilt pattern. The theory that the crazy quilt was the first type of quilt made by colonial women is repeated in book after book and was probably started by quilt historian Ruth Finley. In her 1929 book, *Old Patchwork Quilts and the Women Who Made Them*, Finley wrote:

> In Colonial days, when every finger's wrapping of cloth was brought from Europe in sailing vessels at almost prohibitive cost, each scrap left from the cutting of clothing was worth as much as its equivalent in the garment itself. Thus the "Crazy Patch," fitted irregularly together so that not a thread of the valuable material was wasted, came into being.[2]

Finley's book merely touches on the topic of the crazy quilt, and most later quilt books give crazy quilts the same brief treatment, often using Finley's book as a source. Finley gives no evidence to support her claim, and, in fact, no pre-nineteenth-century crazy quilt, or evidence of one, is known to exist. Her theory, therefore, seems based on the supposition that the scarcity of cloth would lead to every scrap's being used, and none being thrown away. The very process of making a crazy quilt, however, requires more than fabric scraps. A large piece of whole fabric (or at the least, strips or quilt-block-size squares of fabric) is needed for a foundation. The odd-shaped scraps are sewn to this foundation until the foundation fabric is completely hidden. (Imagine a bulletin board entirely covered with pieces of paper and you'll have an idea of how the scraps cover the foundation in a crazy quilt.) This foundation fabric is a necessary part of the quilt top as long as the edges of the fabric scraps are irregularly shaped, as irregular scraps cannot be matched easily at the edges and seamed together. If, however, the scraps are slightly trimmed so that their edges are straight, they can be joined directly to one another without the use of a piece of whole fabric as a foundation. Although there is no proof, it seems logical to consider the possibility that the earliest American quilts were not crazy quilts, requiring additional fabric for foundation pieces, but scrap quilts made of squares, strips, or rectangles that could be pieced together without an additional fabric backing.

What would the fabric scraps left from trimming edges straight be used for? One possibility is suggested by quilt historian Sally Garoutte. According to Garoutte, tiny odds and ends of cloth might well have been used to stuff mattresses. These mattresses, or beds, were usually filled with anything handy: feathers, if possible, but if need be, leaves, corn husks, cattail down, ends of yarn, or odd bits of cloth.[3]

In any case, whether or not the crazy quilt was the original American quilt type remains unproven. It is clear, though, that the crazy quilt as we know it developed and reached its height during the last quarter of the nineteenth century.

Construction of Crazy Quilts

A typical late-nineteenth-century crazy quilt was made by sewing fancy fabric scraps such as silk and silk plush onto a larger piece of lighter-weight foundation fabric. The raw edges of the scraps were usually, though not always, turned under and were held in place by a row of fancy hand-sewn embroidery stitches. The scraps could be sewn to the foundation by sewing machine, but in general this method was not recommended for fear of adding too many straight lines ("angularities offending the eye"[4]) to the finished design. Curves were in fashion; straight lines were out. One set of magazine instructions even suggested avoiding straight lines by overlapping square scraps or cutting off their corners.

The size of the foundation backing determined whether the quilt would be made up of square blocks or long strips or would be made all in one piece. If a quilt was to be put together from small blocks of crazy work, efforts were often made to hide this fact and make it appear as though the quilt had been constructed on one large foundation piece. Embroidery was suggested to conceal straight seam lines where one block met another. If embroidery was not enough, appliqués of curved scraps could be used to cover some of the seams.

Some of the earliest instructions for making crazy patchwork, appearing in women's magazines of 1882, suggested placing a plain square of fabric in the center of the quilt. This square was to be filled with an embroidered bouquet, or with the monogram of the quiltmaker. A different method was suggested in the following year, 1883. Several magazines announced the "new" strip method of making crazy patchwork. "A new and easy way to piece a crazy quilt," suggested one source, "is to cut the strips about a quarter of a yard wide, and then have alternate strips of plain silk or velvet."[5]

The Word Crazy

Using the term *crazy* to refer to a random, irregular pattern in needlework occurred as early as 1878, when readers of the *Cultivator and Country Gentleman* were instructed to buy a square of embroidery canvas and pass it among their friends. Each friend was to embroider whatever design she wished. "When it comes back to you," the newspaper wrote playfully, "you will think it a 'crazy' cushion indeed."[6] This is one use of the word *crazy*: odd, bizarre, irregular, strange, or unusual (all valued attributes in late-Victorian times, as we shall see). It was even suggested, somewhat tongue-in-cheek, that crazy patchwork may have originated among the inmates of insane asylums.[7] Or if this were not the case, possibly the bewildering techniques involved in making the quilt might drive the maker crazy.[8] This meaning of the word *crazy* did not escape the attention of writers and advertisers of the period. "Be careful 'to take your time,'" one magazine advised quiltmaking readers, ". . . and not become 'crazy' to finish it."[9] Advertisers took advantage of the emphasis of bold print and wrote, "**DON'T GET CRAZY** quilts started until you see the new book 'crazy stitches' . . ."[10]

A second meaning of the word *crazy* refers to the odd shape of the individual fabric patches making up the finished design. These pieces were "crazed"—irregularly broken up—in the same way as is crazed china, whose glaze is cracked in an irregular pattern, or crazy pavement, composed of randomly cut stones. (It's also interesting to note that chunks of ore are broken up into smaller pieces in a crazing mill.[11]) Although *crazy patchwork* was the name by which the style eventually came to be known, it was at times also known as *puzzle patchwork*, *Japanese patchwork*, and *mosaic patchwork*.[12]

Use of Silk in Quilts

Before the mid-nineteenth century most quilts were made of cotton or wool. Silk was generally expensive because the hand labor involved in weaving silk thread into cloth made silk manufacturing unprofitable in the United States until silk production became fully industrialized. By 1874, over $21 million worth of silk fabric was being produced in the United States. This was just slightly under the amount being imported into the country at that time. Quilts, quite naturally, reflected the new availability of silk. "Silk has superseded all material less rich and costly," declared *Harper's Bazar*.[13] And *Godey's Lady's Magazine*, as early as 1855, lamented, "Patchwork quilts, unless in silks, are rarely seen in cities, the glory of our grandmothers having passed away."[14] Cotton and wool quilts continued to be made during this time, of course, but by the last quarter of the nineteenth century, they were considered hopelessly old-fashioned.

The patterns that were popularly made up in silk were designs that had an allover focus, rather than an emphasis on individual blocks. Often one geometric form such as a hexagon, a diamond, or a rectangle was repeated to form the entire design. Patterns made of strips, such as Log Cabin, were popular. Bright colors were played off against darker colors, giving an effect not unlike the rich mosaics, tapestries, and stained glass popular in the interiors of the time. By the end of the 1870s, however, something seems to have changed the design of the silk quilt. Rather than patterns composed only of carefully cut geometric shapes, we see, in the crazy quilt, an abandonment of geometry altogether: "We have quite discarded in our modern quilts the regular geometric design once so popular. . . . Now we are very daring. We go boldly on without any apparent design at all."[15]

What caused this shift in taste from symmetrical, regular, geometric designs to the random, asymmetrical irregularity of the crazy quilt? One explanation may lie in one of the major design influences during that period: the growing fascination with the Oriental, and particularly with anything Japanese. It's possible that the intentional "craziness" of the crazy quilt, with its overall patterning of random, asymmetrical patches, was based on a Japanese design.

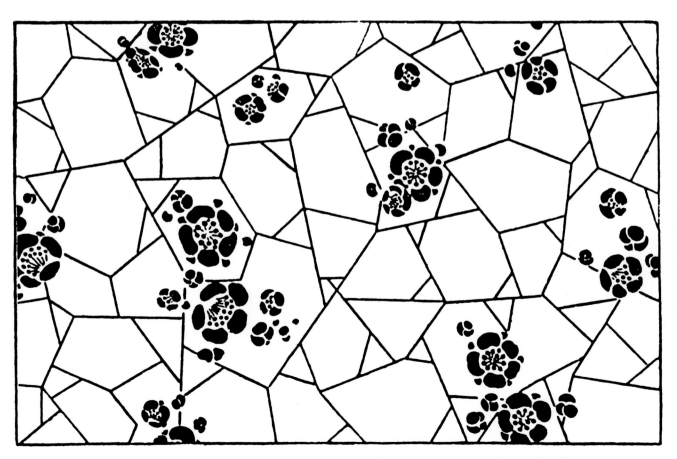

3. Japanese "cracked-ice" design, taken from the book *Pattern Design* (1903), by English designer Lewis F. Day.

Japanese Influence

Several sources from the 1880s repeat the story that the crazy quilt originated as an imitation of a Japanese picture. One of the sources, *Harper's Bazar*, wrote that the idea for "mosaic patchwork of odd bits"—what they called "Japanese Patch"—was taken from the pattern of uneven pavement under a priest's feet shown in a panel of Japanese needlework.[16] This story was repeated a year and a half later by the British magazine *The Queen:* "It is said that the idea for the crazy quilt is to a certain extent Oriental, some Japanese picture, in which was a sort of 'crazy' tesselated pavement composed of odd fragments, having suggested it."[17]

It is possible that a particular Japanese screen, or group of screens, exhibited at the Centennial Exposition in Philadelphia (1876), provided the asymmetrical design influence that came to maturity in the crazy quilt. Some of the screens exhibited there were described as being covered with textured gilt paper ornamented with patches of various materials that had painted, embroidered, or quilted designs.[18]

Whether or not a certain Japanese picture gave the broken, irregular patching design for the crazy quilt is anyone's guess. Another guess is that the Japanese

4. Crazy-patchwork block with painted Oriental characters. One Japanese authority has suggested that although these characters seem to have been written by someone practiced in calligraphy, the translation doesn't make any sense. 1880-1900, 14″ × 14″. (Collection of Betsy Oliphant)

"cracked-ice" design, very popular during the late 1870s and early 1880s, was responsible for the irregular patterning of the crazy quilt.[19] At any rate, it is obvious that the taste for Japanese design accounted in large part for the late-nineteenth-century passion for asymmetrical design in all of the arts, including needlework. Suddenly beauty became equated with the irregular, and adjectives such as *bizarre, strange,* and *odd* conveyed approval and a sense of Oriental mystery. One fashionable magazine noted this, declaring, "Nothing matches or is regular nowadays."[20] Homes were decorated so that every chair was of a different shape and color. There was dinnerware designed with the pieces for each course, from soup to dessert, different in shape and pattern. Even the word *Japanese* came to be synonymous with asymmetry. One magazine columnist summed up the mid-1880s as a time when "The taste is for the gorgeous; Japanese confusion, which is at heart the highest artistic order, reigns."[21]

The primary source of this interest in Japanese design can be traced to direct contact with the Japanese art and artifacts shown at the Centennial Exposition and other later displays. The Japanese Pavillion at the Centennial Exposition was one of the most popular at the fair, and was seen by nearly 9.5 million people. It literally introduced Americans to Japanese arts and culture, with which Americans had had little contact before the exhibition. Part of the Japanese exhibit showed everything from lacquered trays and cabinets, carved wooden furniture, painted and embroidered screens, and silks, to samples of grasses, wood, native animals, and birds. One reporter described his reaction to the displays: "We have been accustomed to regard that country [Japan] as uncivilized at the best, but we find here abundant evidences that it outshines the most cultivated nations of Europe."[22] It is interesting to note that some Japanese influence came to us secondhand from English designers who may have picked up an interest in Japanese design as early as 1862, the year of the International Exhibition in London, which was the first large-scale display of Japanese art outside Japan.

Suddenly an interest in Japan took America by storm and anything Japanese became the latest rage. Tiffany's used Japanese robes and temple hangings as a store display in 1878. Women's magazines printed stories on life in Japan,[23] and advertisements for such novelties as Japanese fans and paper mats ("each mat is very handsomely decorated with curious Japanese designs—3 for 18¢").[24]

Fabric and wallpaper designs reflected this Japanese influence. As early as 1853, a cotton print based on Japanese fabrics was designed. By 1880, fabrics with Oriental designs were highly fashionable. According to a description in *Godey's*, some of these fabrics had "the

5. Detail from wallpaper printed in the 1880s. Notice the circular scene asymmetrically partitioning sections with Japanese vases; owls in foliage sprays; and a view of Coney Island. (Courtesy Cooper-Hewitt Museum, the Smithsonian Institution's National Museum of Design)

6. Detail from crazy quilt, c. 1880–1900 (see fig. 40). This asymmetrical crazy-patchwork block has a superimposed circular scene much like the one in the wallpaper above. (Collection of Marcia and Ronald Spark)

most *bizarre* patterns in the Chinese and Japanese style, and in the brightest coloring over dark or light grounds. Hieroglyphics, chimeras, flying dragons, impossible birds and fishes, are represented."[25]

Designs to be painted or embroidered onto crazy quilts could be taken from fabrics such as these, or from fans, or from scrolls, all of which were widely available at this time. An even more direct Japanese influence can be seen in the Japanese-inspired designs for fancywork printed in women's magazines. *Peterson's Magazine,* for example, featured a page of "Birds from Japanese Designs: In Painting or Embroidery" in 1883, noting that "the superiority of the Japanese in designs of this kind, as also in designs for flowers, foliage, etc., is universally conceded."[26] Oriental designs shown in magazines included scenes of cranes standing in pools of water that were edged with cattails; owls or peacocks perched on gnarled tree branches; swallows in flight; kimono-clad figures of Oriental men and women; folding and paddle-shaped fans; teapots, cups, vases, and bowls; paper lanterns; spiders in webs; and insects and butterflies hovering over flowers such as iris, branches of appleblossoms, and especially chrysanthemums (the national flower of Japan owing to its popularity, which originated because of the emperors' practice of holding annual chrysanthemum displays). The use of these Japanese-inspired motifs spread as they, along with many non-Oriental designs, were offered through the mail.

The Home and Its Decoration

In order to understand fully how the crazy quilt developed, and why it so caught the public fancy, it is necessary to look at the attitude toward home decoration in the late nineteenth century.

The home, in Victorian times, was seen as "the place of Peace; the shelter, not only from all injury, but from all terror, doubt, and division."[27] The responsibility of establishing and maintaining this place of peace and shelter was given to the housewife. Primary among her duties was home decoration—an awesome task in an age believing that elegant and tasteful surroundings could rub off on family members, enriching them spiritually as well as visually. (The opposite was also held to be true. As one woman phrased it, "An ugly, dingy, unattractive, humdrum home never did produce an aspiring, beautiful soul."[28]) It was woman's solemn duty to provide a home worthy of her family, and lack of money, time, or energy did not excuse her from this responsibility. As one interpreter of taste rather harshly sermonized,

> What woman *has* done, a woman *can* do; and we hold that any woman of ordinary strength, and enjoying an

7. Victorian drawing room, Moulton residence, 2119 Calumet Avenue, Chicago, last quarter of the nineteenth century. (Photograph courtesy *The Quilt Digest,* San Francisco)

8. Miss Moulton's room, Moulton residence, Chicago. The unusual quilt on this bed is made of small stuffed squares of crazy patchwork. (Photograph courtesy *The Quilt Digest,* San Francisco)

average of usual health, may by management of details, and judicious expenditure of time, make for herself and those she loves a home, beautiful in embellishment, and furnished with comparative luxury.[29]

Home decoration, therefore, was a chore often tackled with great relish, and at the same time with a bit of fear. To guide them, women had access to magazine articles on decorating, along with an increasing number of books on interior design. These were full of judgments on what was and was not tasteful, and they offered do-it-yourself instructions for creating elegant knickknacks and bric-a-brac by garnishing everyday household objects with the proper arrangement of beads, fabric, thread, lace, paint, feathers, dried weeds and flowers, shells, moss, seaweed, and even taxidermically stuffed animals. By gluing broken eggshells to bottles, for example, a patient woman could imitate the cracked glaze of a rare Chinese urn. Wastebaskets could be transformed by festoons of braid and tassels. The results of all this decorative labor came to be called *fancywork*, which provided every woman with the means of furnishing her home in a suitably splendid manner.

Fancywork

There were fancywork projects for every purpose, real and invented. Negligee pockets were constructed to hold nightgowns that would otherwise be crudely stuffed under pillows; washstand mats, called *splashers*, were embroidered with fitting mottoes ("Rather Wet, Sir") and served to protect the wall behind washstands from water damage; wall pockets kept sitting rooms, halls, libraries, and bedrooms tidy by holding items such as magazines, dustcloths, letters, and hairbrushes that needed to be within reach, but that would add to the clutter if left out ("Not that a little graceful confusion is unpleasant to the artistic taste"[30]).

Fancywork was popular partly because it was a means of making something out of nothing. Frugality was as admired as it was, in many cases, necessary. "In spite of the generally received opinion of the extravagance of women," wrote one columnist in a needlework magazine, "every worker feels a keen sense of pleasure in knowing that she has made good use of material that would otherwise be wasted."[31] *Harper's Bazar* praised the woman who could make "artistic wonders out of hoop-skirts, straws, ravellings of unbleached muslin, scraps of leather, pine cones, old kid gloves, rags—anything, in short, which to the baser sort were rubbish and disgust."[32] The word *artistic* in the preceding quotation is an important one. Women were lauded for having the ability to see the artistic possibilities in scraps and trash. Not only were they creating something out of nothing, but in the process, they were seen as making artistic statements that linked them with the arts-and-crafts movements of the day. Women were reassured that their items of fancywork were "not Trifles but *arts* that, elevating human feeling above animal instincts, make men and women better and families happier."[33]

For women wealthy enough to employ servants to do much of the housework, fancywork became an artistic time-filler at a time when it was a generally accepted idea that all idle moments should be occupied. "If you can't talk and work too," women were admonished, "let the talking wait."[34] Work was seen as the cure for boredom, nervousness, and assorted women's complaints. "The cheerful people are the industrious ones," one magazine declared, warning, "It is the idle who are most subject to fits of melancholy."[35] A needlework magazine called fancywork "the best and only rest possible to many a nervous woman." They couldn't resist adding a note to husbands: "Remember, monsieur, she has not the resource of a cigar."[36]

9. Crazy-patchwork wall pocket, c. 1880–1900, 15″ × 15″. This wall pocket was made by covering a bamboo fan with crazy patchwork. Photograph by John Kluesener. (Collection of Ellen and Dewey Fuller)

Not all late-nineteenth-century women were in the enviable position of having idle hours to while away. For many women then, as now, life was hard. For them, needlework served as a relief from the grim reality of never-ending chores. Notice the last sentence in this letter from an Ohio woman describing a typical day in her life:

> Arose at half-past four, got breakfast for seven persons, washed the dishes, made the beds, swept two rooms upstairs, scrubbed, scoured tinware, chairs and benches, scrubbed the porch, and whitewashed the ceiling, and was done before 11 o'clock. I did not get dinner, but washed the dishes, scrubbed another porch, churned, worked in the garden awhile, got supper for six, washed dishes, fed chickens, gathered the eggs, fed three calves, milked two cows, strained the milk of five, washed the milk buckets, and trimmed a hat before going to bed. Will someone send a pattern for a camp case?[37]

Farm women seem to have been just as interested in fancywork as women from large cities; the interest was the same, but the fabrics available differed. One woman somewhat defensively declared, "Of course we farmers' girls and wives know that in cities, satins and plush are used for fancywork." She added that these materials would be out of place in a farmer's home and suggested that inexpensive materials such as canvas, cardboard, and muslin be tastefully decorated to add to the beauty of the home.[38] Another woman echoed her sentiments: "Fancywork is very nice for those who can afford it, but poor folk like use [sic] who live in a log-house cannot afford so much silk and plush and satin, etc. Would like something to be made out of scraps of flannel."[39]

Fabric Scraps

Whether women had scraps of wool, cotton, or silk, the crazy quilt was seen as the perfect answer to the question of what to do with them. Women's magazines spread the idea that fabric scraps "need not be thrown away or sold to the ragman or sacrificed to the insatiable flames."[40] Instead, they suggested, use these leftover bits of fabric ("silks, ends of ribbons, old waists, discarded flounces, babies' sashes, gentlemen's neckties"[41] and other trims, braids, and beads) to make crazy patchwork.

If no leftovers were available, they could be purchased. Boston's Jordan, Marsh & Co. department store, for example, offered packages of fabric squares by mail for one dollar, stating: "Our tremendous silk-business affords us the opportunity to make this liberal offer, owing to unavoidable accumulation of remnant pieces. Our assortment represents some 300 or more colorings, and each package contains no two alike."[42]

Friends often contributed to the making of crazy quilts by donating finished quilt blocks (in the spirit of album quilts) or by trading scraps. If no fabric was available to offer in trade, anything, within reason, might do. One writer to *The Ohio Farmer* offered to send the pattern for a coat, pants, and collar to anyone who would send her pieces of silk, velvet, or any dress goods suitable for a crazy quilt.

Women appear to have made crazy patches even from the small fabric samples that department stores and silk manufacturers offered to potential buyers. This practice may have been widespread, for the Fall–Winter Montgomery Ward Catalogue of 1894–1895 warned sample orderers that while fabric samples would be sent upon request, these would be in such small pieces as to make them useless for fancy or crazy patchwork.

Another way that crazy-quilt-makers were possibly discouraged from using fabric samples in their creations was suggested in a short story that ran in the July 1884 issue of *Godey's*. The story, called "The Career of a Crazy Quilt," concerns the efforts of the heroine, Heloise, to gather enough fabric to make a quilt. She asks for samples at her local department store: "He gave me quite a lot, lovely pieces, some four inches square," she told a friend. She went on:

> . . . but would you believe it? They were every one pasted on bits of cardboard, so that I couldn't use them at all. Of course I was just too mad for anything! When I asked him what they did that for, he said that they were obliged to because there were some ladies—he supposed they called themselves ladies—who were mean enough to come there for samples when they didn't want to buy anything at all, but just used the silks for patchwork.[43]

By 1884, silk manufacturers sought to profit from the demand for odd bits of fabric and trim and, in doing so, must have had quite an impact on the popularity of the crazy quilt through their promotion of the quilt as a scrap project. One company, the Yale Silk Works, even billed itself as the originator of the silk patchwork craze, but there is no evidence to support this claim. A typical magazine ad from that year reads, "We will mail odds and ends from work rooms—just the thing for 'crazy patchwork.'"[44] Another manufacturer explained its sale of scraps:

> At the time the crazy-work fever broke out, we had accumulated an immense quantity of pieces of plushes and satins, which resulted from the manufacture of the Mosaic work or plush appliqué, and of various fancy articles. . . . The "Craze" gave us an opportunity to dispose of what would otherwise be almost wasted.[45]

Soon competition forced firms to embellish their scraps a bit with the addition of offers of books on crazy patchwork, or even by creating prepackaged kits for crazy blocks. As one such kit was described:

> We put up packages which have advertised themselves so well, that the demand must soon exhaust the supply. At first the packages were not very uniform, some containing more than others, or a better variety of colors, but we have now systematized their make-up so that they will always contain the same number of pieces, variety of colors, etc.[46]

Another kit consisted of "ten *Samples of elegant silk*, all different and cut so as to make one 10-inch block of *Crazy Patchwork*, for 25 cts.; 12-inch block 35 cts."[47] Included in the kit were instructions on how to fit the pieces together to make a block.

While 1884 seems to have been the peak year for the crazy quilt as far as advertisers were concerned (with

10. Crazy patchwork kit, advertised in "Bentley's Catalogue of Novelties in Art Needlework, Stamping Patterns, Lacework &c. 1884–1885." Bentley's described this fifty-cent kit: "contains at least 15 pieces silk plush, 6 pieces satin stamped, (every piece a different shade), and one piece of satin, with small spray embroidered in silk floss. Two sheets of fancy stitches. . . . Our 'B' packages are much superior to anything of the kind offered elsewhere for twice the money, but 50c. is a small sum, and it is evident that the plushes furnished for that amount, cannot be cut from new goods." (Photograph courtesy Missouri Historical Society)

11. Examples of crazy-patchwork blocks made from Bentley's kit, shown in "Bentley's Catalogue of Novelties in Art Needlework, Stamping Patterns, Lacework &c. 1884–1885." (Photograph courtesy Missouri Historical Society)

12. Designs suggested for crazy-patchwork blocks, from *Crazy Patchwork*, a pamphlet published by Strawbridge & Clothier, Philadelphia, 1884. This pamphlet was offered free to new subscribers to Strawbridge & Clothier's *Fashion Quarterly*. (Illustration courtesy Irma Koski)

eight ads for silk for patchwork in the May 1884 issue of *Peterson's Magazine*, for example), firms were still offering fabric scraps by mail into the 1890s. Even after the passion for the crazy quilt had completely cooled, there were still offers of silk scraps illustrated with drawings of crazy-quilt blocks. Possibly the last advertisement of this type appeared as a full page in the January 1935 issue of *Comfort Magazine*. The offer was for a package of "patchwork silk" plus needles and instruction book in exchange for two new subscriptions. The magazine claimed that all the silk had been collected from silk factories. As they described it, "Under the cutting table are boxes to catch the remnants and waste. Every bit of it is fresh, new silk. It seems so dreadfully wasteful!"[48]

Decorating the Patches

The patches in crazy quilts could be left plain, but they were often decorated with paint and embroidery. Only rarely, however, were the painted and embroidered designs completely original. Most came from patterns that were printed in magazines or they could be purchased. The patterns were generally perforated, traced, or transferred.

PERFORATED PATTERNS

Perforated patterns had holes punched in an outline of the design. Many varieties of these patterns were offered by mail in ads such as this one, which read: "50 perforated paper patterns including: sprays of golden rod, pansies, wild roses, Forget-me-nots, thistles, strawberries, Outlines of Boy, Girl, Bugs, Spiders, Storks, Crazy stitch patterns, pond lilies, tulips."[49]

Women wanting to make their own perforated patterns could easily trace a design onto paper—or use the original design itself—and then poke holes into the paper following the lines of the design. (This method explains why one sometimes finds old issues of women's magazines in perfect condition—with the exception of a few pages of designs that are full of holes.) The holes could be made by hand with a needle, or with the needle of an unthreaded sewing machine. For two dollars one could even buy a gadget called the Little Wonder, which purported to perforate ten sheets of patterns at once. There was also a sewing-machine attachment that would make holes that were supposedly smooth on both sides of the paper (making both sides of the pattern usable). The manufacturer explained that each hole was made by "actually removing an atom of the paper the size of the needle or punch used."[50]

Perforated patterns were easy to use. They were simply placed on the right side of the fabric being marked and held there while stamping powder was forced through the holes in the pattern. A fabric pad, called a *pounce* or a *poncet*, held the powder and was used to powder the pattern in much the way that a powder puff is used. When the powdered pattern was lifted up, an outline of powder dots remained to guide the embroiderer. These powder dots were often joined with a line of black or white paint before they became smudged. The marked design was then ready to be filled in with embroidery stitches or with more paint.

Perforated patterns were so popular that in 1885 the *Ladies' Home Journal* magazine offered twenty-five as a premium to readers bringing in sixteen new subscribers. They packaged these patterns in a "Crazy Patchwork Outfit," consisting of twelve prestamped pieces of silk; one box of stamping powder with pounce; twelve skeins of embroidery silk; and "a glittering array of 2 dozen spangles and 2 yards of tinsel cord."[51]

TRACING AND TRANSFERRING THE DESIGN

Many women simply traced a design from a book or magazine and transferred it onto fabric. They could do this easily by using a soft lead pencil or crayon to trace the design and then placing the tracing face-down on the fabric. When they went over the lines, pressing hard, the crayon or lead marks were transferred to the fabric.

There was also transfer paper available that would leave a mark when drawn upon, as well as designs that were already marked on paper and could be transferred to fabric with a hot iron. Women's magazines

13. Iron-on transfer for crazy-patchwork block, from *Crazy Patchwork*, published by Strawbridge & Clothier, Philadelphia, 1884. (Illustration courtesy Irma Koski)

sometimes printed their fancywork designs on this iron-on transfer paper so that women could rip them out and use them.

For women who were less than confident of their abilities or would rather not bother with marking, some firms offered fabric patches already stamped with designs. Their stamping may have left much to be desired, however, as one irate customer complained, "The Crescent Art Co., Revere, Mass., are not what their advertisement would lead one to expect. They sent me . . . a small patch of cotton velvet about four inches square, on which there was a stamped pattern (very poorly stamped) that only an artist could have understood or painted."[52] Once the design was marked the fabric was ready to be embroidered or painted.

EMBROIDERY

Women's magazines, along with manufacturer's crazy-quilt instruction booklets, commonly gave instructions for a few basic stitches that could be used to embroider any design. Three of these stitches were the outline stitch, the Kensington stitch, and the plush stitch.

OUTLINE STITCH

The outline stitch, often called the *stem stitch* today, was perhaps the most common stitch used to form designs on crazy quilts. Used by itself, it forms a thread line—much like a line in a drawing. Outlined designs continued to be popular even after the crazy quilt went out of favor. They are still used, often as red outlines against a white cotton background.

KENSINGTON STITCH

The Kensington stitch is not one particular type of stitch, but a free and painterly way of applying colors of thread, in stitches of irregular length, so that the colors blend into one another and imitate areas of paint on canvas. On crazy quilts, it was used basically to fill in outlined designs. The name *Kensington stitch* came from the Royal School of Art Needlework in the South Kensington district of London.[53]

PLUSH STITCH

The plush stitch produces a textured area of cut silk threads—much like a short pile on a carpet. It was done with strands of a silk thread such as filoselle (an inferior silk not suitable for regular embroidery). Short strands of filoselle were laid on top of the design and held in place by a stitch of embroidery thread. The strands were then clipped short so that they would stand up straight, making a fuzzy pile.

EMBROIDERY STITCHES ALONG SEAMS

In addition to stitches that were used to make embroidered designs, rows of embroidery were used along the edges of patches to decorate them and at the same time to hold the raw edges under and in place. One set of instructions gives some idea of the variety of these stitches:

> Join the edges with cat-stitch and brier-stitch, or with any of the great variety of fancy stitches; such as coral-stitch, single, double, and triple; border-stitch; herringbone; button-hole, over and under; cross-stitch; chain stitch, single and double; French knots; and point russe of every style.[54]

Brier stitch was another name for the feather stitch, the most common of the edge stitches used.

EMBROIDERED APPLIQUÉS

For those women without the skill, the time, or the inclination for embroidery, there were preembroidered appliqués, which could be purchased and sewn onto crazy-quilt patches. Some were machine-embroidered and could be moistened on the back and pressed onto the fabric with a hot iron. As one manufacturer boasted, "When these ornaments are properly applied they look almost as well as the nicest hand embroidery on the material." Their machine-made appliqués were, they added somewhat snidely, "a good deal better than anything the average woman can achieve in the way of silk embroidery."[55] This may well have been their opinion, but a decorating magazine held a different view. While these appliqués were extremely fashionable, they said, "many of them are not particularly beautiful."[56]

For women with more taste than time, at least one company provided hand-embroidered sprigs of flowers ready to apply. The embroidery was done on net and when the appliqué was sewn onto a quilt patch, it appeared to have been hand-embroidered. The convenience of these embroideries did not come cheaply, however. While a 4½-inch single rosebud with three leaves could be had for fifty cents, a 16-inch rose spray (made up of two open roses and one half-open rose in pink, crimson, or yellow, with seven buds and twenty-four leaves) cost a whopping six dollars. (By comparison, a skilled laborer in 1880 earned an average daily wage of $2.26.) No wonder they advertised prominently that every flower sprig would arrive carefully packed in a separate box.

PAINTING

Painting on fabric was a popular pastime and was used to decorate screens, curtains, panels in window shutters, fancywork items, and even clothing, in addition to crazy-quilt patches. Some women created original landscapes and portraits of family members or pets, and some saw painting on the fabric patches as a quick alternative to embroidery. "I painted flowers on some of the blocks; they are much prettier than embroidery and not so much work," one woman wrote.[57]

Those who wanted a painted effect quickly could use sheets of paper that had been specially printed with oil-color designs. These could be moistened and transferred to fabric by pressing with a hot iron.

During this period, a method called *Kensington painting* was developed in an attempt to imitate the stitching in Kensington embroidery. Kensington painting was quite different from other methods of painting because it was usually done with a pen rather than a brush. The pen was turned over so that paint could be scooped up and held in the hollow of the pen point as it was drawn across the fabric. This technique deposited paint on the fabric in thick lines resembling stitches. Smaller "stitches" were scratched in with the pen tip or a needle. Manufacturers were quick to take advantage of the popularity of Kensington painting by introducing pens with three, five, or seven points—made especially for scratching the paint. A full Kensington painting kit, consisting of thirty tubes of oil paint, brushes, palette, pens, and a sample of work, could be ordered for six dollars.

OTHER DECORATIONS

RIBBON

Ribbon was used on crazy quilts in a wide variety of ways. Wide ribbons became quilt patches. Narrower ribbons could be twisted and sewn as braid would be. Still narrower ribbons were gathered and sewn into three-dimensional flower petals. Ribbon remnants were available from manufacturers, just as were fabric and embroidery thread scraps. One advertiser offered "Fancy Ribbon for Crazy Patchwork," consisting of twenty-five pieces of assorted ribbons, two to five inches wide, for fifty cents.[58]

BEADS

Beads, sequins, and spangles were often used on English crazy patchwork, where the combination of braid work with bugle beads was known as *Belgravian embroidery*. Beads show up less often on American crazy quilts, and when they do, they are normally used to form designs such as flowers or bugs, rather than being randomly scattered as they are in English crazy work.

METALLIC THREAD

Metallic thread, called *Japanese gold thread*, was made with gilt paper wound around cotton thread. It had the advantage of never tarnishing. Real gold and silver metal, cut into thin strips and wound around cotton thread, was called *French* or *English gold thread*. To keep it from tarnishing, one source recommended that it be wrapped in paper containing cloves.

Metallic braid is found particularly in English crazy work. A description of how it was to be used on crazy patchwork suggested laying it on the finished patchwork in loops and swirls: "the more it curls, twists, and 'meanders' about the better. The appearance should resemble the plans of a maze or labyrinth more than anything else."[59] For a design to be considered truly successful, not more than an inch of patchwork was supposed to show between the metallic thread lines, and even these spaces were meant to be filled with embroidery.

Godey's, in February 1881, called gold thread the "great feature of the embroidery of the season."[60]

THREE-DIMENSIONAL FORMS

Motifs were sometimes stuffed from behind to become three-dimensional. This was a revival of a seventeenth-century needlework technique called *stumpwork*, in which forms of animals, birds, butterflies, fruit, and flowers were stuffed, backed with paper, and sewn to a background fabric (see fig. 56).

English Crazy Work

Crazy patchwork appears to have been an American invention—a "peculiarly American" quilt, in the words of one English writer, who, in 1884, described the first crazy quilt that she had seen as looking like some piece of Oriental fabric.[61]

Two years later, at a time when American women had been familiar with crazy patchwork for years, the English magazine *Girls' Own Paper* was just introducing its readers to the quilt style:

> Those whose time is much occupied with household matters, and who cannot devote much time to the task of making their drawing-rooms pretty, we recommend to try crazy patchwork. . . . The work is one of the least expensive that can be tried, and can be put down without derangement of effort at any moment.[62]

Judging from the crazy patchwork now in English museums, English crazy work tended to be used on small fancywork items as often as on large quilts. Items such as smoking caps, slippers, tidies, cushions, and tea cozies turn up in museums in England more frequently than they do in the United States. (This cir-

14. Crazy-patchwork mat, 1880–1900, 5½″ × 9″ (excluding fringe). This mat is a perfect example of the English winding-braid technique used on crazy patchwork. (Collection of Worthing Museum, Worthing, England)

15. Pair of slippers (mules), last quarter of the nineteenth century, 9″ long. (Collection of Museum of Costume and Textiles, Nottingham, England)

cumstance may, however, merely reflect different museum-collection policies.) Both the small pieces of fancywork and the large quilts of the English show differences in style from American crazy work. These differences are in the use of gold thread, braid, beads, and embroidery.

The use of winding lines of metallic braid and scattered beads in English work has been briefly discussed earlier. Generally, the English did not share the American concern for keeping decoration within the boundaries of the patch. Not only do beads and lines of braid cross from one patch to another, but it is common to find embroidered designs extending across several patches. Often the brocade design of one patch is continued in embroidery on a neighboring patch—just as if the brocade extended across the boundaries.

This combination of braid, beads, and embroidery blurs patchwork lines and creates a very rich, textured, overall effect in English crazy work.

Everything Gets a Little Crazy

After the initial novelty of the crazy quilt wore off in America, "craziness" began to show up in other forms of fancywork, sometimes in an obvious imitation of the crazy quilt's random effect. Meandering lines of embroidery, for example, were used to divide pieces of plain fabric or geometric patchwork into crazy sections. This false crazy-sectioning can sometimes be seen in block-style crazy quilts that combine plain squares with blocks of crazy patchwork. Possibly it was used as a quick way of getting a crazy effect without going to all the work of appliquéing scraps to a foundation.

Other scrap fancywork projects also developed at this time. A rug made with carpet remnants, the center being "filled in every color . . . all mixed in 'hilter-skilter,'" was described by one *Ohio Farmer* reader.[63] Crazy socks were knit, and crazy afghans crocheted, from balls of yarn made by tying together odds and ends of yarn. Even gardening was affected. "Have any of you tried making 'crazy beds,' mixing all kinds of flower seeds together and planting them in a bed?" wrote an Ohio woman. "They look very pretty and it is something new, and odd."[64]

Possibly the strangest idea suggested by crazy quilts appeared in *The Ladies' World* magazine in 1890. The magazine announced to its readers, "Crazy quilts, pillows, etc., are going swiftly 'out,' but crazy teas are a new and very pleasant diversion."[65] The theme of a crazy tea was to be made plain from the moment that the guests received their invitations, for these invitations were to be written in various colors of ink on cards of different shapes and sizes and were then to be stuffed into envelopes that didn't match. The guests, arriving at the stated time, would find the hostess's home suitably decked out with crazy quilts ("nearly everyone has friends who will lend them") hung on the walls and draped over doors. Pictures were to be turned upside down and rehung on the walls. Sofas were to be covered with books, vases, and fancywork (making the guests sit on the floor?). Lamps, topped with shades of all colors and sizes, were to be placed in out-of-the-way corners. The guests who were not fortunate enough to have eaten recently were treated to the following menu: baked beans covered with currant jelly, cornbread and cheese frosted with chocolate icing, tarts stuffed with chow-chow, and, to quench the resulting thirst, hot, salted lemonade. Even the party conversation (assuming anyone was still able to talk after a few sips of lemonade) was to be made "crazy" by being stopped and redirected to a new topic every five minutes, at the sound of a bell rung by the hostess.

16. Patchwork block with random lines of embroidery imitating crazy patchwork. The October 1884 issue of *Arthur's Home Magazine* suggested embroidering the ends of towels in irregular sections to give the look of crazy work. (Photograph courtesy Dorothy Beers and Bev Rush)

Crazy Fabric

Fabric design also reflected the period's interest in crazy effects. At least one design for cotton fabric was printed to imitate crazy patchwork—complete with the popular motifs of butterflies, a swallow, two owls, a fan, flower sprigs, and a huge spider in a web, as well as a roller-skating boy, a racket and balls, the head of a dragon, a hive circled by bees, and a paisley cone design.

Another type of fabric inspired by the crazy quilt was called *crazy cloth*. It was made with a permanently crinkled surface that probably bore little resemblance to a crazy quilt, although it was broken up into irregular sections.

18. Advertisement for crazy cloth, from *Harper's Bazar,* March 6, 1886, p. 166.

17. Fabric printed to resemble crazy patchwork, 1886. Photograph by Jim Birr and Tim Branco. (Courtesy Nancy Ray)

A Crazy-Quilt Show

Quilt shows featuring crazy quilts appear to have been popular during the 1880s. The story of one such show (mentioned at the beginning of this book) emerges slowly from the pages of *The New York Times* in the winter of 1885:

November 6, 1885: "A Crazy Quilt Show"
Over 300 entries, consisting of nearly 2,000 items, had been received for the National Crazy Quilt and Needle Art Exhibit to be held at the Masonic Hall on November 17. Some of the entries were made by men, and the manager of the exhibition, one Fred Kyle, was heard to comment: "In former exhibitions of this kind some of the handsomest work has been contributed by gentlemen." Gold and silver medals as well as cash prizes amounting to $3,000 were to be awarded. Among the categories to be judged were the largest crazy quilt, the quilt with the greatest number of pieces, the quilt with the greatest variety of stitches, and those with the oddest designs and the oddest materials.

November 18, 1885: "Exhibiting Crazy Work"
"People who have recently passed the Masonic Temple . . . have been startled by seeing on either side of the main entrance of the building posters bearing in large and lurid red letters the word 'CRAZY!.'" Among the entries was a crazy table cover by Mrs. C. Y. Bogert containing 4,000,000 stitches.

December 6, 1885: "The Crazy Quilt Show"
Ninety-eight prizes were announced, but the show itself was judged to be a financial failure. Contributing to this situation was the unforeseen expense incurred, due to the fact that every Saturday evening the Masonic Temple had to be totally cleared of the exhibits to make way for the Sunday morning meetings of the Manhattan Temperance Association.

December 30, 1885: "Looking for Mr. Kyle"
Several prizewinners were "anxiously seeking the present whereabouts of Mr. Frederick Kyle." The Gorham Manufacturing Company was also looking for Kyle who had ordered 110 medals with the words "Crazy Quilt Show" stamped on one side. While it had been announced that over 800 prizes were to be awarded, "this must be looked upon as a pleasant little fiction, invented as a gilded bait to lure on owners of crazy quilts." Kyle, known as an organizer of bird, cat, dog, and baby shows, was not available for comment.

Anti-Crazy-Quilt Sentiment

While many women felt the grip of crazy-quilt mania, others ridiculed the practice of "forming absurd patterns of tiny scraps." Antifancywork crusaders generally fell into one of two camps: those who felt the close work to be an unhealthy strain on eyes and nerves, and those who felt it a complete waste of time better spent on other pursuits. Into the "it's unhealthy" group fell this sharp-tongued writer:

19. Sickafoose pillow, by Mrs. A. Sickafoose, Lyons, Iowa, 1893, 20″ × 20″. This crazy-patchwork pillow with designs of embroidery and petit point was sent in a wooden box with pink cambric lining to the Chicago World's Columbian Exposition of 1893. It reportedly was a prize winner at that fair. Photograph by Ed Gross. (Collection of Joyce Gross)

I know of several ladies who have so far overtaxed their eyesight as to require complete rest for a long time, with loss of power which may be permanent, and all for a piece of work which is quite useless. . . . I have a hopeless sort of pity for the woman who says, "I am saving up silks for a crazy quilt." . . . But I suppose it will be a great pleasure to say to the grandchild who inquires as to the origin of the odd combination, "Yes, my dear, I lost my eyesight while working on that very thing. But it is a great satisfaction to me to feel of it now."[66]

A more serious, and perhaps justified, argument was that fancywork could be a time waster, placating women who might better use the time to improve their minds. "There is too much talk about fancy work," wrote an *Ohio Farmer* reader with the nom de plume of Miss Jumbo. "Fold up your fancy work, lay it aside for awhile, and come out and have a chat on something that means business. . . . Will someone please tell me how to make chow-chow?"[67]

Another writer estimated that at least one quarter of

the work performed by women was unnecessary, "like the ottoman cover I once saw a lady working." She went on:

> She was all bent up and putting her eyes out counting stitches. She had spent more time embroidering a ridiculous dog . . . than I had spent with my books in a year. . . . To fill time, to pass it busily, is not to use it. . . . Delicate work that ministers to no human need, even if it has artistic merit to recommend it, if it consumes the hours a woman ought to use training her mind to think and her eyes to see . . . is but busy idleness and a waste of time.[68]

Another writer applauded the sentiments expressed above, adding, "An intelligent, well read woman makes home more beautiful than all the fancy work ever made."[69]

Women's magazines were overwhelmingly in favor of crazy quilts, with a few exceptions. Under the column heading "Crazy Work and Sane Work," a *Harper's Bazar* writer called the labor spent on crazy quilts "misdirected energy and perseverance too common among women." The writer estimated that making a quilt of nine thousand scraps (allowing ten minutes per scrap) would take fifteen hundred hours, or one hour a day for more than four years. The suggestion was that this amount of time might be better spent in more intellectual pursuits.[70]

The Decline of the Crazy Quilt

The life of any intensely popular fad is short. At the peak of interest in the crazy quilt, around 1884, one can see a glimmering of renewed interest in the traditional pieced and appliquéd quilt styles that the crazy quilt had temporarily eclipsed. In July 1884, one magazine reported, "Old patterns, and modifications of old ones, are continually coming to the front in silk quilts, so that when the crazy quilt has had its day there will be plenty of styles to supplant it."[71] Many of these silk quilts—fan designs, Log Cabins, Baby Blocks—were made without any random, crazy-quilt patches, but they are often confused with crazy quilts because of the heavy embroidering along their seams.

The basic cotton patchwork quilt, in low esteem throughout the late 1870s and early 1880s, outside the rural areas, began the road to rediscovery. The *Ladies' Home Journal* declared, "The decree has gone forth that a revival of patchwork quilts is at hand."[72]

After approximately 1910, there was little widespread interest in the crazy quilt. The very characteristics that so appealed to women of the 1880s—asymmetry, the strong contrasts of color and texture, and the lavish use of fabrics and trims—made the crazy quilt seem bizarre, old-fashioned, and overly decorated to the more modern eyes of the early twentieth century. Crazy quilts continued to be made, but they were commonly made of wool, or even cotton, and although the random patching was maintained, the rich and elaborate surface decoration was usually absent. The crazy quilt of the twentieth century became primarily utilitarian rather than decorative.

Conclusion

Recent trends in contemporary art and architecture have created a cultural environment ripe for the reevaluation of the crazy quilt. Ever since the late 1960s, there has been an increasing movement away from the clean, bare, geometric style of some modern art and architecture, toward a renewed interest in ornamentation and the designs of the past. Interior designers, for example, who formerly created interiors with stark white walls, leather chairs, and tables cleared of all evidence of human life are now filling rooms with flowering plants, baskets, quilts, folk art, patterned wallpaper and fabric, and painted furniture. Architects now borrow freely and with tongue-in-cheek from the architectural styles of the past. Old buildings that formerly might have been stripped of all ornamental detailing, or even torn down completely, are being thoughtfully restored. The items of "junk" of past years are now called *collectibles*—including everything from comic books, political buttons, and Mickey Mouse watches, to salt and pepper shakers and cap guns. And crafts that have been dormant for years, such as the making of stained glass, furniture, decorative ironwork, and handmade paper, are vigorously coming to life again.

Along with this decorative tendency in architecture, interior design, and the crafts, there is a new ornamentation occurring in fine arts. Artists are reaching beyond themselves and their immediate environment for subject matter and are finding inspiration in the designs of such traditionally "low-art" sources as ethnic art, basketmaking, wallpaper and pottery designs, tilework, and women's needlework, which includes lace making, crocheting, quilting, and embroidery. In their own personal response to these designs, artists often use materials and motifs that are similar to those found in crazy quilts: materials such as light-reflective beads, sequins, and metallic thread; paint on fabric; and the motifs of flowers, birds, butterflies, animals, pottery, and fans.

What this new ornamentation in the arts means for crazy quilts is a chance for them to be seen in a new context. The past ten years have seen the development

20. *What Is Paradise II*, by Miriam Schapiro, 40½″ × 31¾″. Fabric and acrylic paint on paper. The rich swirling patterning in this contemporary painting recalls the profusely decorated crazy quilts of a century earlier. (Courtesy Barbara Gladstone Gallery, New York City)

of a passionate interest in quilts in general—but particularly an interest in quilt styles such as pieced-block designs and Amish quilts. These quilts reminded collectors, critics, and curators of the then-current geometric paintings with large simple shapes and grid designs. The decorative tide has now turned away from strict geometric designs. It is moving toward a lush patterning, evocative of other times and places, rich with contrasts of texture, color, and line. It is in the light of this new interest in the richness of ornamental patterning that the merits of the crazy quilt can now be seen.

Not all crazy quilts are beautiful, or even interesting. The pieced quilt has the stylistic safety net of geometric repetition to fall back on, making even the least remarkable pieced design interesting if only for its predictable repetition of geometric shapes. But the crazy quilt has no such safety net. It is, in its way, the precursor of collage. Its artistic success depends not on repetition but, in most cases, solely on the artistic sensibility of the quiltmaker.

The crazy quilt reached the height of its popularity exactly one hundred years ago. It is time to look at the crazy-quilt style with a fresh eye. This book attempts to show the wide variety of forms that crazy patchwork has taken, and how, more than any other quilt style, the crazy quilt reflected and had an effect on the period in which it was made.

A Closer Look

21. Crazy-patchwork pillow shams, by Julia Chappell Skillman, Connecticut, 1886, 30″ × 30″ each. (Collection of Oregon Historical Society)

22. Crazy quilt, signed Mrs. M. James, Kentucky, 1887, 78½" × 68½".
(Collection of Helen and Robert Cargo)

23. Embroidered medallion head, detail from crazy quilt (see fig. 35, p. 36), c. 1880, Bucks County, Pennsylvania. This head is a slight variation of that shown in fig. 24. (Collection of M. Finkel & Daughter, Philadelphia)

24. Medallion head, embroidery design from *A Lady's Book*. This design is from page 33 in a book of fancywork designs called *A Lady's Book*, published by M. Heminway sometime after 1876. The text with the design reads, in part, "The accompanying design is one of the very latest, and is becoming so popular we take pleasure in presenting it. . . . This style of

design is more particularly adapted to tidies, table covers and scarfs [*sic*]." (Courtesy Center for the History of American Needlework)

25. Embroidered sumac design, detail from crazy quilt by Katherine Wells Codding, 1880–1900. The fuzzy flowers of the sumac are done in plush stitch. Photograph by John Kluesener. (Collection of Alta and Charles Codding)

26. "Sumach Design for Scrim Tidy," from *The Delineator*, July 1883, p. 41. Photograph by John Glascock.

Patterns

Many of the designs for flowers, butterflies, spiders, and so on that were used on crazy quilts can be traced back to their original sources: printed patterns found in women's magazines, books on fancywork, or manufacturers' and department stores' brochures.

BOOKS AND MAGAZINES

All of the leading women's magazines, including *Godey's, The Delineator, Harper's Bazar,* and *Peterson's,* printed embroidery patterns. These patterns were designed for use on tidies, table scarves, linen towels,

handkerchiefs, wall pockets, and other types of fancywork in addition to crazy quilts. The pattern for sumac leaves and flowers (fig. 26) from *The Delineator,* for example, was originally meant to decorate a cotton or linen tidy (a mat used on chairbacks or arms to keep the chair clean). The use of a variety of fancywork patterns from magazines partly explains why the scale of designs in crazy quilts often varies considerably from patch to patch—a huge flower, for example, next to a tiny owl. This size difference might also mean that the quilt was a group effort. Books of fancywork patterns

27. Embroidery-stitch patterns, The Brainerd & Armstrong Co., c. 1885. This may be the earliest source of these embroidery patterns. The Brainerd & Armstrong Co. manufactured embroidery thread, and these patterns were offered as incentives to women ordering thread. (Courtesy York Institute Museum, Saco, Maine)

were another source of crazy-quilt motifs. The medallion head design (fig. 24) is from *A Lady's Book*, published after 1876. A variation of this head (fig. 23) is found on a crazy quilt made around 1880, possibly by a Quaker church group.

FABRIC AND THREAD MANUFACTURERS
Companies manufacturing thread or fabric offered brochures showing decorative ways to make use of their scrap waste. One thread company, Brainerd & Armstrong, advertised their sheet of "designs for 100

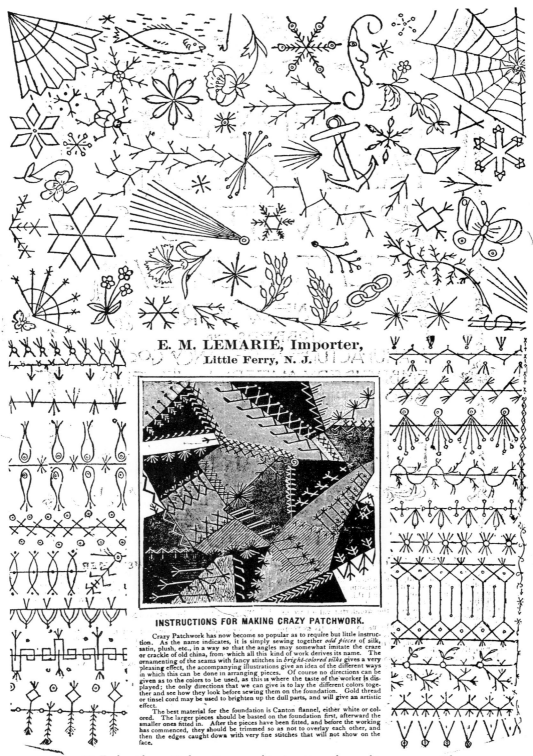

E. M. LEMARIÉ, Importer,
Little Ferry, N. J.

INSTRUCTIONS FOR MAKING CRAZY PATCHWORK.

Crazy Patchwork has now become so popular as to require but little instruction. As the name indicates, it is simply sewing together *odd pieces* of silk, satin, plush, etc., in a way so that the angles may somewhat imitate the craze or crackle of old china, from which all this kind of work derives its name. The ornamenting of the seams with fancy stitches in *bright-colored silks* gives a very pleasing effect, the accompanying illustrations give an idea of the different ways in which this can be done in arranging pieces. Of course no directions can be given as to the colors to be used, as this is where the taste of the worker is displayed; the only directions that we can give is to lay the different colors together and see how they look before sewing them on the foundation. Gold thread or tinsel cord may be used to brighten up the dull parts, and will give an artistic effect.
The best material for the foundation is Canton flannel, either white or colored. The larger pieces should be basted on the foundation first, afterward the smaller ones fitted in. After the pieces have been fitted, and before the working has commenced, they should be trimmed so as not to overlay each other, and then the edges caught down with very fine stitches that will not show on the face.

28. Embroidery-stitch patterns and instructions for making crazy patchwork, E.M. Lemarie Company, 1897. These designs are identical to those offered earlier by Brainerd & Armstrong. Notice that the right side of the sheet is cropped from the spider on down the page. Some of the edge stitches on the bottom half of the Lemarie page are eliminated to make room for the sketch and instructions for crazy patchwork. (Courtesy M. Finkel & Daughter, Philadelphia)

styles of crazy stitches'' as an incentive to customers ordering packages of thread ends, or what they called "Waste Embroidery." The designs on this sheet—spiders' webs, anchors, butterflies, bugs, and so on—often show up on crazy quilts. It's impossible to say that the Brainerd & Armstrong sheet was definitely the source of these designs, however, for the identical designs were sent out by other manufacturers, even into the 1900s.

PATTERNS FOR QUILT BLOCK DESIGNS

There were also patterns showing how to make crazy-patchwork blocks from scraps. These block patterns were, like designs of bugs and flowers, copied and reissued by different companies, over a period of ten or fifteen years. These block patterns probably served more as inspiration to crazy-quilt-makers than as actual designs to be copied, but at times they were followed quite closely.

29. Crazy-patchwork mat, Pennsylvania, initialed *L.S.*, 21½'' × 21½'', c. 1885–1900. It is clear that this mat was embroidered following designs from printed patterns. In addition to the musical staff, there are the familiar anchor, sprig of flowers, butterfly, interlocking rings, and umbrella, also seen on the previous pages. (Collection of Kiracofe and Kile, San Francisco)

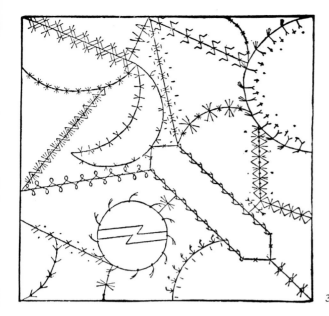

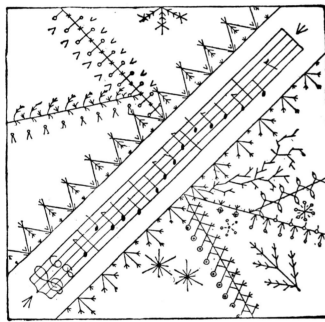

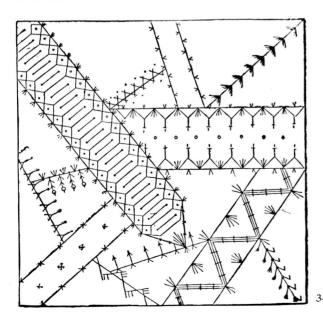

30. Design for crazy-patchwork block from *Ornamental Stitches for Embroidery*, published by T.E. Parker, Lynn, Massachusetts, 1885. The musical staff in this design is not identical to the staff embroidered on the crazy-patchwork mat in figure 29, but there is a striking similarity between the two designs. (Collection of York Institute Museum, Saco, Maine)

31. Detail of crazy quilt, signed Mrs. M. James, Kentucky, 1887. (Collection of Helen and Robert Cargo)

32. Design for crazy-patchwork block from *Ornamental Stitches for Embroidery*, published by T.E. Parker, Lynn, Massachusetts, 1885. The similarity between this block design and the patchwork block in figure 31 is too close to be coincidental. It is quite probable that the design from this block was transferred to a square of foundation fabric and served as a guide for making the crazy-patchwork block. (Collection of York Institute Museum, Saco, Maine)

33. Detail of crazy quilt, signed Mrs. M. James, Kentucky, 1887. Notice how similar many of the embroidery lines are to those in the pattern in figure 34. (Collection of Helen and Robert Cargo)

34. Design for crazy-patchwork block from *Ornamental Stitches for Embroidery*, published by T.E. Parker, Lynn, Massachusetts, 1885. This design, with its narrow crisscrossing bands, would be ideal for using up bits of ribbon and dress trim. (Collection of York Institute Museum, Saco, Maine)

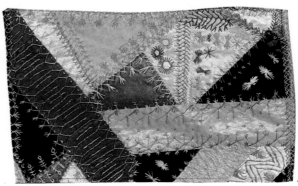

Construction

Crazy quilts come in the same varieties as do other quilts: they were made in one piece; they were made in blocks, strips, and diamonds; and sometimes they were even made to form designs such as stars or hexagons. The quilts were generally tied or tacked (tied, with the ties showing on the back rather than on the front) because the velvets and plushes used in making the quilts were too heavy to quilt through. Sometimes a machine-quilted backing was used on a quilt.

ONE-PIECE, OR RANDOM, DESIGN

Quilts made on one large piece of foundation backing were generally started in the center or at one of the corners. Patches were added randomly, without any overall design's being planned out beforehand.

35. Crazy quilt, Bucks County, Pennsylvania, c. 1880, 55″ × 53″. This quilt belonged to a Quaker family and may have been made by a church group. Most of the embroidered patches contain the initials of the person who decorated them. The quilt is a good example of a random arrangement of patches on a large foundation backing. (Collection of M. Finkel & Daughter, Philadelphia)

36. Scrap screen, illustrated in *The Delineator*, April 1884, p. 289. Scrap screens, especially popular in 1882–1883, were made by covering standing or folding screens with overlapping scraps of paper or fabric. They bear an interesting resemblance to randomly arranged crazy quilts. Photograph by John Glascock.

37. Crazy quilt, by Ann Jenkins (1856–1950), Croston, Rhoose, Glamorgan, Wales, 1895, 60″ × 63″. The small, randomly placed patches in this Welsh quilt make it resemble a mosaic or a stained-glass window. Yellow embroidery thread forms the intricate, intertwined flower design along the lower edge of the quilt. It looks as if the quiltmaker started to stitch the same design along the upper edge of the quilt, beginning at the center, but decided against it and used the simpler and less time-consuming crisscross pattern instead. (Collection of National Museum of Wales [Welsh Folk Museum], St. Fagans, Cardiff, Wales)

38, 38a. Crazy quilt with bouquet center medallion, 1884, 51″ × 51″. Many of the flowers on this quilt are embroidered appliqués, although there are many more, including the central bouquet, that have been done by hand directly onto the quilt patches. A small cream patch (near the piece embroidered with the year 1884) shows two chickens fighting over the same worm and is labeled "this little chicken won't divide with her sister." Photograph by John Kluesener. (Collection of Lillian Buckholts)

39, 39a. Silk and velvet "table cover" with central panel, c. 1880–1900, 59½″ × 59½″. We generally use the term *crazy quilt* for all pieces of crazy patchwork, but many of these "quilts" were actually made to be table or piano scarves. Others were made to be used as bed quilts, or as "slumber robes" to keep the chill off daytime nappers. (Collection of Helen L. Allen Textile Collection, The University of Wisconsin–Madison)

CENTRAL MEDALLION

Central medallion crazy quilts are either random patch quilts, with a strong design in the center, or block crazy quilts with a dominant center block. The quilts are often square in shape.

40. Crazy quilt with monogrammed central medallion, c. 1880–1900, 58″ × 58″. Many of the velvet patches on this quilt are hand-painted with moonlit scenes, flowers, chicks hatching, a cat's head, and even rackets and balls. Photograph by Tom Burk. (Collection of Marcia and Ronald Spark)

BLOCKS AND STRIPS

Making quilts of small blocks and strips of crazy patchwork was not as cumbersome as trying to work on the whole quilt at once by covering a large foundation backing from one end to the other with small scraps. Block-style crazy quilts were probably the most common type of crazy quilt, although sometimes the fact that a quilt was made in blocks was intentionally obscured by the sewing of patches over the block seams.

41. Sampler crazy quilt, c. 1885, 39″ × 52″. A diagonal row of crazy blocks runs through the center of this quilt. Note the plain black blocks given a crazy effect with random lines of embroidery. Photograph by Tom Burk. (Collection of Marcia and Ronald Spark)

42, 42a. Crazy quilt embroidered with paisley cone designs, c. 1900, 65″ × 65″. This uniquely beautiful quilt was undoubtedly inspired by the paisley shawls that were so popular earlier in the century. Lines of embroidery in swirls, dots, and crosshatchings fill the monochromatic patches and make this quilt an exquisite example of the Oriental richness in turn-of-the-century decorative art. Photograph by John Kluesener. (Collection of Mr. and Mrs. Albert J. Silber)

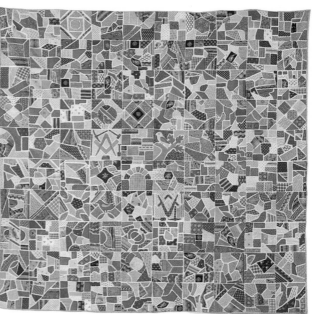

43. Log Cabin with crazy block and border, signed J. Berg and A. Riecke, dated 1879 and 1884, 64″ × 70″. The border, generally the last part of a quilt to be made, was probably done in crazy patchwork during the height of the crazy-quilt fervor. The crests in some of the blocks may have been made from the silk liners found inside men's hats. Photograph by John Kluesener. (Collection of Mr. and Mrs. Albert J. Silber)

44. "Tile" crazy quilt with Masonic symbols, last quarter of the nineteenth century, 85″ × 84″. Photograph by John Miller. (Museum of Our National Heritage)

45. Strip "tile" crazy quilt, 1876–1900, 64" × 74". The crazy patches in this quilt are appliquéd to cream-colored strips. The patches appear as "tiles," with cream "grout" embroidered with stars, lines, and branches of feather stitching. (Collection of Mary Strickler's Quilt/Linda Reuther and Julie Silber)

DIAMONDS

The diamond, based as it is on diagonals, is a more active shape than the square, which rests solidly on a firm foundation. Crazy quilts made with diamond-shaped blocks often have a very lively look and almost seem to twinkle.

46. Contained crazy quilt, cotton, Amish, from the Phineas Borntrager family of Amherst, Wisconsin, c. 1930–1945, 96″ × 72″. This quilt has been grouped with other diamonds because of its appearance. It is actually made of square blocks, each of which has a diagonal stripe of black down the center. The crazy patchwork in each block appears to have been pieced together, with no scrap too small or too irregular to include. (Collection of M. Finkel & Daughter, Philadelphia)

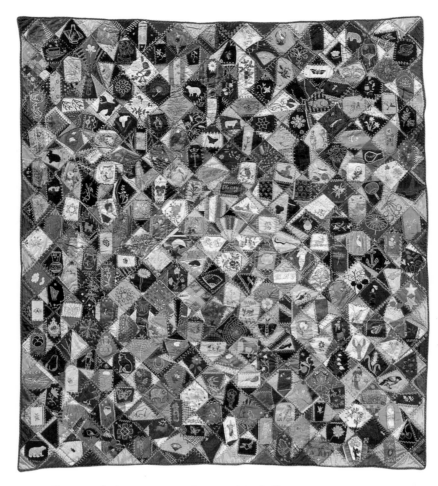

47. Crazy quilt, by Victoriene Parsons Mitchell (1829–1916), 1883–1893, 84½'' × 73''. The phrase "One could spend hours looking at it" is literally true of this amazing quilt. No matter how many times one looks at it it always reveals something new. Some of the stranger motifs stuffed in among the usual birds and flowers are a rat with a black-jet bead eye, a rabbit-drawn wagon driven by another rabbit, a lobster, a naked cherub with wildly fuzzy hair, and a wonderfully bizarre scene of a spiderweb in which a woman dangles upside down. (Collection of Indianapolis Museum of Art; Gift of Mrs. Jaema C. Ryan)

48. Contained crazy quilt, cotton, Lancaster County, Pennsylvania, last half of the nineteenth century, 86″ × 79″. It's a "which came first, the chicken or the egg" question with this type of crazy quilt. Contained crazies such as this one are often estimated to date from the 1860s, which would probably make them the earliest existing crazy quilts. The dates are open to question, however, and quilts of this type may have been made after the Centennial Exposition with fabric dating from the 1860s. (Collection of M. Finkel & Daughter, Philadelphia)

HEXAGONS

Quilts made with tiny hexagons of silk or cotton were very popular during late Victorian times, especially in England. This popularity of the hexagonal shape shows up in crazy quilts that have hexagons formed of crazy patchwork.

49. Pieced and embroidered crazy quilt, c. 1890, 86″ × 80″. This marvelous crazy quilt has diamond-shaped crazy patches joined to form hexagons. The hexagons are separated from one another by black triangles, which, if looked at in just the right way, become star points. Take a close look at the flowers along the red velvet border. They appear to have been copied from patterns of flower sprigs and are repeated to form the long garlands. (Collection of Connecticut Historical Society)

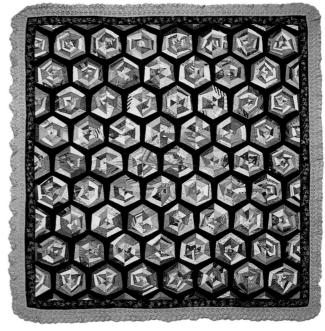

50. Pieced crazy quilt, c. 1880–1890, 53″ × 57″. The hexagons making up this quilt were pieced from triangles. The triangles were also pieced, for the most part, from irregular strips of fabric. Quilts made with thin strips in this way are sometimes called *string quilts.* (Collection of Seneca Falls Historical Society, Seneca Falls, New York)

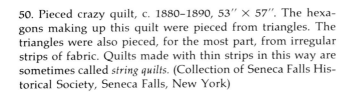

STARS

The star has always been one of the best-loved images in quilt design, and one sometimes sees crazy quilts made either with crazy patchwork stars on a plain background or with plain stars against a field of crazy patches.

51. Crazy quilt with central basket and stars, c. 1884, initialed M. S. M., 72″ × 67″. The pieced stars set into crazy-patchwork blocks make an elegant border for the busy central medallion of this crazy quilt. Included in the quilt's center, along with the basket of woven ribbons, are a Blaine–Logan campaign ribbon (1884), a horseshoe studded with beads and sequins, an American flag, and a pansy in a cornucopia, along with those roadside rivals, the tortoise and the hare. (Collection of Lorain County Historical Society Museum, Elyria, Ohio)

52, 52a (opposite). Touching-stars crazy quilt, by Lizzie Rock Edwards, Schoeneck, Lancaster County, Pennsylvania, 1896, 81″ × 80″. The crazy star points, combined with the embroidered motifs of flowers and butterflies and fancy edgestitching along the seams, clearly show a late Victorian influence at work. (Collection of M. Finkel & Daughter, Philadelphia)

53. Crazy stars, Elverson, Pennsylvania, c. 1880–1890, 66″ × 65″. Plain star shapes are set against a background of crazy patchwork. Notice the fanlike shapes near the center of the quilt, and how the quilt ties, which are done in a variety of colors, give a twinkling effect. (Collection of M. Finkel & Daughter, Philadephia)

54. Mrs. L. W. Bliss and animals she mounted in her home in Crandon, Wisconsin, c. 1900. Imagine how great a task stuffing a peacock would be, with that great tail of feathers to wrestle with. From the looks of this living room scene, no animal was safe in the vicinity of Mrs. Bliss's home in Crandon. Dare we wonder what happened to Mr. Bliss? (Courtesy of State Historical Society of Wisconsin)

Motifs

BIRDS AND BEASTS

Winged, finned, and four-footed friends were not only popular subjects for quilt motifs but, when stuffed, served as objets d'art, adding that necessary odd touch to the decor. Both wild and domestic animals were used, and household pets were sometimes memorialized in this way. One woman, for example, wrote of preserving "friends of the family," such as faithful old Carlos the dog and the "gleeful warbler Dickie," in a glass cabinet. She placed this cabinet in the library—making, in her words, a "household ob-ject of unusual interest and beauty, which calls forth the admiration of all who see it."[73]

The popularity of home taxidermy during the 1880s was great enough to warrant several articles on the subject in fashionable magazines such as *Harper's Bazar*. One of these articles discussed in detail the process of stuffing a bird and ended with a warning: "the greatest care must be taken during the whole operation not to stretch the skin, or the form of the bird will be spoiled."[74]

55. Crazy quilt by Mrs. David McWilliams, c. 1882, 84" × 84". Mrs. McWilliams made this quilt for a raffle held in 1882 to benefit the Mullanphy Hospital. Typical fans and flowers appear on the quilt, but they were obviously not enough for Mrs. McWilliams, who added two taxidermically stuffed chipmunks at the bottom to give her quilt that unique finishing touch! (Collection of Missouri Historical Society)

56, 56a, 56b, 56c. Crazy quilt with animals, made by Florence Elizabeth Marvin, Brooklyn Heights, New York, 1886, 80″ × 76″. A true animal-lover's quilt! Along with such whimsical details as a stuffed glove and two cavorting cherubs, this wonderful quilt is a menagerie made up of four horses; fifteen owls; six stags; one chicken and twelve roosters (two carrying brooms); four goats; eighteen butterflies; four grasshoppers; two cows; two turtles; one elephant with sequin-studded blanket; eleven cranes; one rabbit, peacock, pig, camel, dragonfly, spider, frog, cat, fish, and dog; one nest of eggs; and twenty-three assorted birds (including what appear to be two partridges in a pear tree?). (Photograph courtesy America Hurrah Antiques, New York City)

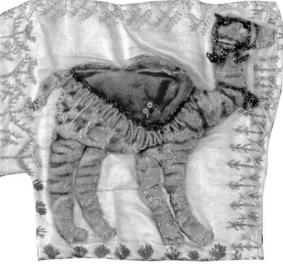

The peacock, with its elegant carriage and splendid plumage, was often used in Renaissance art, sometimes to symbolize vanity. The popularity of the peacock motif reached new heights in the 1870s and 1880s when English designers, inspired by Oriental peacock designs, began using the bird on fabric and wallpaper. The American artist James McNeill Whistler painted lavishly ornate gold peacocks over a blue-green background in his famous decorating scheme for what came to be called the Peacock Room (1876–1877). By the late 1870s, the peacock feather (with its companions the lily and the sunflower) stood for the attribute of beauty, symbolizing the Aesthetic Art Movement in England and the United States. And during the early 1880s, using the feathers in home decor, on clothing, or on crazy quilts demonstrated to others how fashionably modern one was. It is interesting to notice that, by and large, the peacock is always depicted on quilts with his tail down, rather than fanned open, and is usually seen perched on a tree branch.

57. Embroidered peacock, center block detail from a crazy quilt, 1880–1900, 20″ × 20″. Photograph by Tom Burk. (Collection of Ronald and Marcia Spark)

58. Embroidered peacock, lower-right border detail from a crazy quilt, 1884. (See fig. 38.) (Collection of Lillian Buckholts)

59. "We're From the Owl'd Country," detail from a Bucks County, Pennsylvania, crazy quilt (see fig. 35, p. 36), c. 1880. (Collection of M. Finkel & Daughter, Philadelphia)

60. Three owls, detail from a crazy quilt by Flora Henrietta Schille Constans, Ohio, c. 1885. These owls are an example of Kensington painting. (Collection of Ohio Historical Society)

OWLS

The owl is depicted on crazy quilts as a rather comical bird, more a figure to be poked fun at than to be looked up to as a symbol of wisdom. Many playful liberties were taken with the word *owl* in quilt slogans, such as, "Where have you been owl summer?" This is the question that a stern mother owl, perched on a branch with her baby, asks of what is presumably the father owl, who has returned to the branch holding a fishing pole, complete with rodent dangling at the end of the line. Solitary owls, identified as females by the bonnets they wear, are labeled "Owl'd Maid." Another pattern shows two owls above the saying, "We're From the Owl'd Country." *Godey's* advertised an owl pattern in 1884 showing four owls sitting together on a tree branch—each reading an issue of the magazine. The typical owl on a crazy quilt is shown sitting either on a tree branch or on a crescent moon.

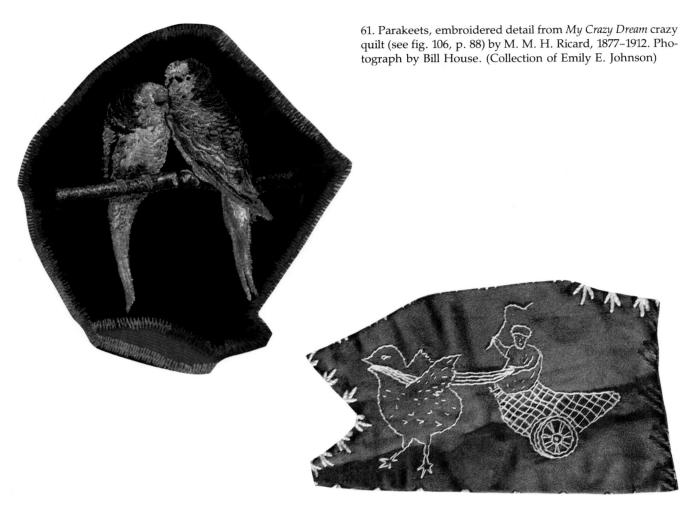

61. Parakeets, embroidered detail from *My Crazy Dream* crazy quilt (see fig. 106, p. 88) by M. M. H. Ricard, 1877–1912. Photograph by Bill House. (Collection of Emily E. Johnson)

62. Bird-drawn chariot, detail from a crazy quilt by Katherine Wells Codding, 1880–1900. Photograph by John Kluesener. (Collection of Alta and Charles Codding)

OTHER BIRDS

The late Victorian fashion of wearing real, stuffed birds on hats and as hair ornaments caused *Harper's Bazar* to editorialize, "A world-wide slaughter of the innocents has been going on to supply birds to satisfy this new caprice."[75] Many of these birds were exotic species from the jungles of South America, but not even lowly pigeons, ducks, crows, and magpies, were entirely safe. If not used on hair and hats, they could become fans: "The head and breast of the bird are stuffed and dressed and the spread wings form the 'fan.'"[76] Bird wings of all kinds were often tucked behind picture frames to add a decorative touch to the room. One woman described having "the large owl, red tail hawk, Cooper hawk (all trophies of the protection of our poultry), duck, curlew, prairie chicken,

black turkey and Brown Leghorn rooster wings. . . . I do not have all those wings in one room, but through the house where they will fit in nicely."[77]

The birds most commonly depicted on crazy quilts, other than the obligatory owls and peacocks, are swallows (always seen in flight), and cranes (often wading in swampy pools with one leg raised high). Country quilts typically show chickens and ducks. Parrots, robins, eagles, doves, and crows are sometimes seen (the latter possibly owing its presence to the popularity of Edgar Allan Poe's poem "The Raven"). But as interesting as the birds that are shown on crazy quilts are, those that are not—bluejays, cardinals, woodpeckers, seagulls, and flamingos—are just a few of the distinctive birds generally left off crazy quilts.

Cats were well-used motifs on crazy quilts (as they were in folk art in general). Their popularity is underscored by the fact that they were used by at least two stamping-pattern manufacturers in advertising copy, as a means of catching the reader's eye. The J. F. Ingalls Company of Lynn, Massachusetts, ran an ad in 1885 that read, "OUR CAT-alogue has over 1700 illustrations of New and Choice Stamping Patterns." In the same year, Bentley's Art Needlework Company used a sketch of a scrawny cat with arched back in their ads, along with the words: "THIS CAT IS NOT VERY PRETTY NOR VERY BIG but we will send you A PRETTY BIG CAT-alogue for 10 cents." Another 1885 Bentley's ad read, "ALL OTHER CATS ARE KITTENS when compared with our new and handsome catalogue issued March 1."

65. Cat head, embroidered detail from a crazy quilt by Katherine Wells Codding, 1880–1900. Photograph by John Kluesener. (Collection of Alta and Charles Codding)

64. Painted cat head, detail from a crazy quilt (see fig. 40, p. 39), 1880–1900. Photograph by Tom Burk. (Collection of Marcia and Ronald Spark)

63. Advertisement from *The Delineator*, June 1885, p. 503. Photograph by John Glascock. (Courtesy of Allen Art Museum Library, Oberlin, Ohio)

66. Cat holding a mouse, detail from a quilt by Flora Henrietta Schille Constans, Ohio, c. 1885. Note the blanket stitches surrounding the cat. These indicate that it is probably an embroidered appliqué, possibly machine-made. (Collection of Ohio Historical Society)

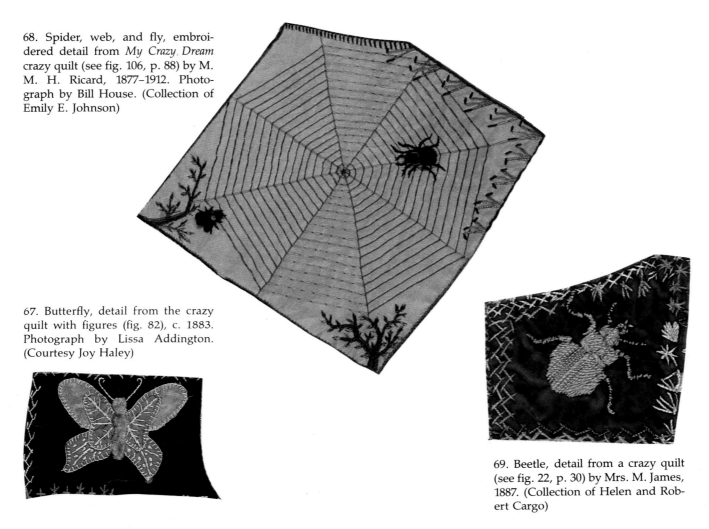

68. Spider, web, and fly, embroidered detail from *My Crazy Dream* crazy quilt (see fig. 106, p. 88) by M. M. H. Ricard, 1877–1912. Photograph by Bill House. (Collection of Emily E. Johnson)

67. Butterfly, detail from the crazy quilt with figures (fig. 82), c. 1883. Photograph by Lissa Addington. (Courtesy Joy Haley)

69. Beetle, detail from a crazy quilt (see fig. 22, p. 30) by Mrs. M. James, 1887. (Collection of Helen and Robert Cargo)

SPIDERS, BUTTERFLIES, AND INSECTS

Spiders, moths, butterflies, and insects of all kinds were used to decorate patches on crazy quilts. They were not a new subject for embroidery: inventories of Queen Elizabeth's wardrobe, for instance, taken in about 1600, mention dresses covered with embroidered spiders, flies, and webs. Nor was the interest in these creatures limited to their use in embroidery. Butterflies were worn during the second half of the nineteenth century on hats and hair, and jewels in the form of beetles, dragonflies, and other insects were popular. Pins were often designed with a somewhat pranksterish desire to fool the eye. *Godey's* told readers, "A fly is the fancy ornament of the day; a pretty little fly, so skillfully and perfectly imitated that it looks like life. . . . It deceives everyone."[78]

Late Victorians seem to have held a special fondness for spiders and their beautiful webs. The Ohio Historical Society has a wonderful hat covered with gold-embroidered spiderwebs, and *Harper's Bazar* tells readers of a spider pin "with its body of pearls and legs of sil-

ver . . . crawling in among the latest novelties."[79] One exotic dancer of the period, Lola Montez, even performed a spider dance. This must have caused quite a sensation, for it involved her plucking off bits of her costume as if throwing off spiders.

At the same time that designers used the spider as a motif, there was an attempt to use the fine, strong thread spun by spiders as a substitute for silk. The major difficulty seems to have been collecting the thread. *Harper's Bazar* described how spiders could be made to emit their thread by being tossed from hand to hand. There were even experiments made with steam-driven engines, which were used to reel up the thread as fast as the spider could spin it out. The article concluded, "the difficulty of rearing a sufficiently numerous family of spiders within a reasonable space, on account of their extreme pugnacity [they tended to eat one another if their appetites were not satisfied with a plentiful supply of flies], soon interfered with this budding industry."[80]

FANS, FLAGS, AND FLOWERS

FANS

Folding fans, imported from Japan by way of China, became popular in Europe in the early 1600s. By 1800, fans were out of fashion, only to be revived as the result of a duchess' whim. In 1827, the Duchesse de Berry planned a ball to be held at the Tuileries. Because one of the dances to be performed was in the style of Louis XV, the duchess decided to use old fans to set the mood. The result was a new rage for fans—a rage that seems to have spread to the United States by the last quarter of the century, when it became the fashion to use palm leaf fans, bound in ribbon and decorated with flowers, as a substitute for bouquets. The craze for Japanese items made the Oriental fan a decorative necessity. Tasteful decors featured fans scattered randomly on a wall or arranged to form borders around the ceiling. This practice was probably influenced by the artist James McNeill Whistler's use of fans as wall decorations as early as 1867. Fancywork items were made with fans and there were even magic trick fans for practical jokers: "Latest thing out . . . hand it to a friend and it instantly falls in pieces; you alone can restore it. Causes endless fun and wonder."[81]

The interest in fans shows up both in block-style quilts, made with fan blocks, and in crazy quilts. Some of the fan designs used on crazy quilts came from patterns, such as a *Harper's Bazar's* page of "Japanese Fan Designs for Embroidery," featured in the August 24, 1881, issue. Other fans were appliquéd in imitation of both folding and paddle-shaped fans. The latter are often shown in pairs, with one fan crossed over the other.

70. Crazy quilt with fans, 1880–1900, 67½″ × 67½″. (Collection of Allen Memorial Art Museum, Oberlin College)

71. Fan, detail from a crazy quilt (see fig. 100, p. 82) with fan blocks by Josephine Dobt Ronnebaum and Anna Maria M. Ronnebaum Kinker, 1894. Photograph by John Kluesener. (Collection of Barbara Kasselmann)

72. Painted, pieced, and appliquéd fans, detail from a crazy quilt (see fig. 109, p. 84) by Mary Schelly Millikin, c. 1883. Photograph by John Kluesener. (Collection of Paul T. Millikin)

73. Crazy quilt with fans, c. 1880, 56″ × 68″. (Collection of America Hurrah Antiques, New York City)

FLAGS

The American flag, shown flat or snapping in an imaginary breeze, was used on all types of quilts and folk art in general. Its popularity probably received an additional boost during the patriotic period surrounding the Centennial Exposition.

In addition to flags, many political campaign ribbons and other souvenirs were saved and sewn onto crazy patchwork in the same way that they would have been pasted into albums twenty years earlier. Many of these ribbons were originally attached to badges given out at such gatherings as political rallies and army reunions.

75. Flags, detail from a mourning crazy quilt (see fig. 105, p. 86), c. 1900. (Collection of Mary Strickler's Quilt/Linda Reuther and Julie Silber)

74. Souvenir flag banner from the Chicago World's Columbian Exposition (1893), detail from a crazy quilt, 1889–1893. Photograph by John Kluesener. (Collection of Mr. and Mrs. Albert J. Silber)

76. Flag, detail from a crazy quilt (see fig. 111, p. 96) by Elvina Harter, 1880–1904. Photograph by Lance Ferraro. (Collection of Peggy Stouck Petrucci)

The flowers on crazy quilts were meant to look as if they'd just been picked. In general, they're less stylized, and look more natural, than flowers on appliqué quilts. They are shown as they grow: in sprigs made up of leaves, stems, and buds in all stages of maturity.

There are fashions in flowers, as in everything else. During the early 1880s, the fashionable flowers were sunflowers, iris, lilies, and cattails—tall, stiff-stemmed flowers. The popularity of these flowers undoubtedly originated in England, where they were used on Royal School of Art Needlework embroideries, which were seen by American women both at the Centennial Exposition and as illustrated in magazines. English designers such as William Morris had used the sunflower design since the 1860s. Along with the lily and the peacock feather, the sunflower became a symbol of the progressive art movement of the day. A prime spokesman for this movement, with its new ideas about art, design, and decoration, was the flamboyant Oscar Wilde, who reportedly wore a lily or a sunflower in his lapel. His warmly received lecture tour of the United States in 1881–1882 inspired American women to create sunflower-filled "Oscar" crazy quilts, as well as such fancywork items as Oscar Wilde penwipers made with yellow flannel petals. By 1885, the sunflower fever had cooled; as *Harper's Bazar* reported, "Few people will be sorry that the sunflower has been weeded out, the cat-tail relegated to its native swamps."[82]

Flowers were also used on quilts for their symbolic meanings. The rose, for example, stood for love; the daisy for innocence; the pansy for remembrance. The Victorians popularized a "flower language," a sort of hidden code by which messages could be sent by means of the right combination of blooms.[83] Each flower was assigned a certain meaning, a meaning that might vary according to which of the dozens of flower language books was consulted. Some of the most common flowers and their meanings are:

Daisy	Innocence
Pansy	Thought, remembrance
Iris	Message
White lily	Purity
Marigold	Grief
Narcissus	Egotism
Red rose	Love
Yellow rose	Jealousy
Full-blown rose over two buds	Secrecy
Violet	Faithfulness
Weeping willow	Mourning

It's hard to say how much intended flower symbolism may be on a particular quilt, and whether the flower is used for its meaning or merely for its beauty. The possibility of these hidden meanings should not be discounted, however, and it certainly adds to the charm of the quilts.

77. Crazy quilt, silk and velvet, dated 1885, 72″ × 56″. Here is a fine example of floral motifs in a crazy quilt. The central basket of flowers establishes the theme, which is then embellished by various sprigs of flowers scattered over the surface of the quilt, together with such grace notes as the flower-bedecked shoe and horseshoe. Photograph courtesy America Hurrah Antiques, New York City. (Private collection)

PEOPLE AND PLACES

Figures of children are more commonly found on crazy quilts than are adult figures. The main reason seems to lie in the embroidery patterns that were available. There were a great number of stamping patterns and transfer designs of children, the majority of which were copies of Kate Greenaway figures (see page 75). Designs showing adults, however, were generally not available, with the exception of some patterns showing women doing such household chores as sweeping or scrubbing at washtubs. In general, then, most embroidered or appliquéd adult figures found on crazy quilts were original designs, while those of children came from patterns.

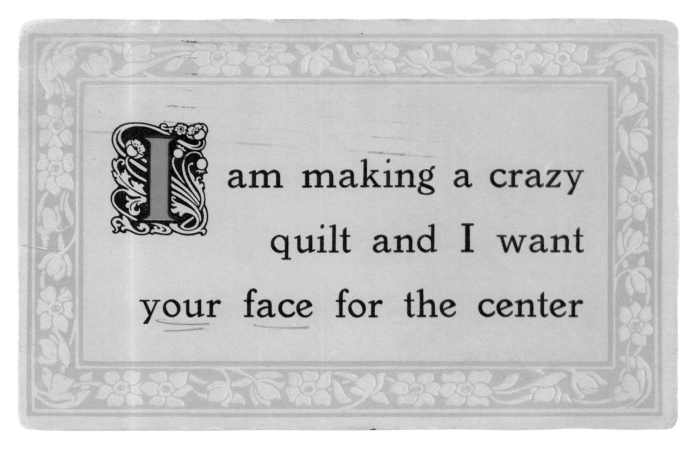

78. Postcard (front). A writer signed "Sis" from Chicago sent this postcard, postmarked October 13, 1911, to Miss Minnie Heald of Davenport, Iowa. Someone, probably the sender, underlined the words "your face" to make sure that the point of the joke was not lost. (Private collection)

79. (Opposite) Crazy patchwork table runner, 1880–1915, 21⅝" × 14". Who is this mystery woman? My guess, which admittedly is a stab in the dark, is that it is the actress Anna Held. Possibly she was featured on a cigarette premium. From about 1910 to 1915, manufacturers of Nebo, Zira, Egyptian Straights, and Tokyo cigarettes gave out ribbons with pictures of kings and queens, actors and actresses, opera stars, Indians, butterflies, and flags—much like the later baseball cards packaged with bubblegum. Women collected these premiums, often using them in quilts. Whoever this woman is, she's not unique to this quilt. So watch for her and you may see her again. (Collection of Helen L. Allen Textile Collection, The University of Wisconsin–Madison)

80, 80a–80k. Crazy quilt with figures, by Leila Butts Utter, Delaware County, New York, 1898, 84″ × 76″. This wonderful quilt features a complete cast of characters, from a dapper Dan in plush polo coat who clutches a briefcase, to a tweedy fellow with a paunch who looks as though he's just overeaten once again. The figures are full of personality; even the way they hold themselves seems to give clues to their character. It's an amusing quilt, with the possible exception of the two blocks showing black children, which are rather jarring caricatures. Photograph by Schecter Me Sun Lee. (Collection of America Hurrah Antiques, New York City)

81. John L. Sullivan crazy quilt, Illinois, dated 1888, 79″ × 76″. The imposing physique of John L. Sullivan, one of the early heroes of American sports, dominates the center of this wonderful quilt. The quilt is dated 1888, but it was probably still being worked on in 1889, when Sullivan battled Jake Kilrain in the last bare-knuckle heavyweight championship boxing contest. Photograph courtesy America Hurrah Antiques, New York City. (Private collection)

82. Crazy quilt with figures, c. 1883. Photograph by Lissa Addington.
(Courtesy Joy Haley)

83, 83a–83e. Crazy quilt with appliquéd and embroidered figures, 1880–1890, 52″ × 52″. Embroidery lines are used to draw in such details as the folds and wrinkles of the women's dresses. This linear treatment suggests that the figures may have been copied from book or magazine illustrations. (Collection of Seneca Falls Historical Society)

84. Crazy patchwork with baby-blocks center, c. 1880–1900, 17″ × 17″. The baby-blocks design is very precisely pieced, while the border of crazy patchwork is rather crudely done. It's possible that they were done by different hands and that the center is a remnant of an earlier piece that was salvaged and made into crazy patchwork. Small pieces such as this are sometimes called baby or doll quilts, but more likely they were intended as table mats. Photograph by John Kluesener. (Collection of Mr. and Mrs. Albert J. Silber)

85. Crazy crib quilt, midwestern United States, c. 1890, 33″
× 46″. (Thos. K. Woodard: American Antiques & Quilts)

86. Thomas baby propped up on a crazy-quilt-covered chair,
c. 1905. (Courtesy of Helen and Robert Cargo)

87. Detail of crazy quilt (see fig. 100, p. 82), ''Little Red Riding Hood and the Wolf,'' Katherine Wells Codding, 1880–1900. Photograph by John Kluesener. (Collection of Barbara Kasselmann)

88. A young girl from North Branch, Michigan, c. 1890, who perhaps helped her mother sew the blocks for this quilt. Needlework projects were considered proper and useful ways to occupy a girl's time. As one young girl noted in her diary, ''Mama made me get my crazy quilt out and embroider on it all morning because she wanted to keep me busy and it was all I could do.''[84] Photograph courtesy Sandra Mitchell.

89. This 1913 book features a live doll made of crazy patchwork. The illustrator was John R. Neill. (Private collection)

Kate Greenaway (1846–1901) was an English artist whose illustrations for children's books had an influence on quilt design. Greenaway was best known for her scenes of children at play, and her practice of dressing the children in her drawings in fashions from an earlier century (based partly on clothing she'd seen as a child in a rural area, where older clothing styles were still being worn) caught the public fancy. Her fame spread to Europe and the United States after her book *Under the Window* was published in 1878. Scenes from that book and others were made into embroidery patterns that were illustrated in American women's magazines. *Harper's Bazar* was probably the first American magazine to print Greenaway drawings. The January 11, 1879, issue contains a scene of children lined up for a dance. This drawing was not labeled as being by Greenaway, but the style and the initials "K. G." on the lower left corner of the picture identify it as hers. The November 1880 *Godey's* ran a page of unattributed embroidery designs—either by Greenaway or closely copied from her work. And both the July 23, 1881, and the January 28, 1882, issues of *Harper's Bazar* printed embroidery designs credited to Kate Greenaway. In addition to these printed designs, there is also a mention made of a "Kate Greenaway quilt." This appeared in the October 14, 1882, issue of *The Ohio Farmer*, along with the suggestion that Greenaway figures be copied directly from her books. By 1883, *Arthur's Home Magazine* called her name a household word, and *Harper's Bazar* spoke of Greenaway designs being used on parasols. It was probably around this time that stamping-pattern companies began offering Greenaway designs for embroidery—many from her book *Under the Window*. Small figures of Greenaway children done in outline embroidery, appliqué, and paint—children shown dancing, fishing, rolling hoops, or just sitting quietly on walls and fences—are common quilt motifs and quite probably served as models for the many later "sunbonnet" children patterns especially popular during the 1920s and 1930s, and again during the 1970s.

90. Child rolling hoop, detail of a drawing by Kate Greenaway, from her book *Under the Window: Pictures and Rhymes for Children*, 1878. Photograph by John Kluesener.

91. Advertisement for stamping patterns, showing Kate Greenaway design of a child rolling a hoop from *Under the Window*. This ad appeared in *Dorcas Magazine*, April 1884, p. 116, and also in the December 15, 1883, issue of *Harper's Bazar*. Photograph by John Kluesener.

92. Child rolling hoop, outline embroidery design, detail of a crazy quilt by Mary Schelly Millikin, c. 1883. Photograph by John Kluesener. (Collection of Paul T. Millikin)

93. Kate Greenaway boy and girl holding hands, embroidered appliqué.(Collection of Cincinnati Art Museum; Gift of Pearl Cotteral)

94. Boy blowing trumpet, appliqué and embroidery. This figure was based on the Kate Greenaway design for the verse "Pipe thee high, and pipe thee low" from her book *Under the Window*. In the original illustration, the boy's trumpet playing accompanies two dancing figures. A variation of this trumpet-blowing boy appeared as a pattern in the July 23, 1881, issue of *Harper's Bazar* and was offered as an iron-on transfer design by Briggs & Co. Detail from crazy quilt by C. Heintz (1827–1916), 1884. (Collection of Cincinnati Art Museum; Gift of Mrs. George D. Newstedt)

95. Two girls sitting on a fence, Kate Greenaway design printed on a ribbon, detail from a crazy quilt by Katherine Wells Codding, c. 1880–1900. Photograph by John Kluesener. (Courtesy of Alta and Charles Codding)

PLACES

Crazy quilts are sometimes based on the image of a
particular place, whether it's a house, a civic building,
or even—as in The Newark Museum's railroad quilt—
a large area made up of towns and countryside.

96. Crazy quilt, by Mrs. A. E. Reasoner, New Jersey, c. 1885, 90″ × 88″. Mrs. Reasoner was
the wife of a railwayman who was the superintendent of what would become the Delaware,
Lackawanna, and Western Railroad. Her design treats the crazy quilt as an aerial map, rep-
resenting the railway route as it passes from Hoboken, New Jersey, through the tunnel and
past the stations of Newark, Orange, South Orange, Summit, Madison, Convent, and Morristown, to arrive at its final destination, Richfield Springs. People are lined up along the
route to watch the train, including a group of four babies that are stuffed into a stroller.
Several horses run on the yellow roads near the tracks, while at the bottom of the quilt
birds fly over a blue silk river that carries large and small boats. (Collection of The Newark
Museum)

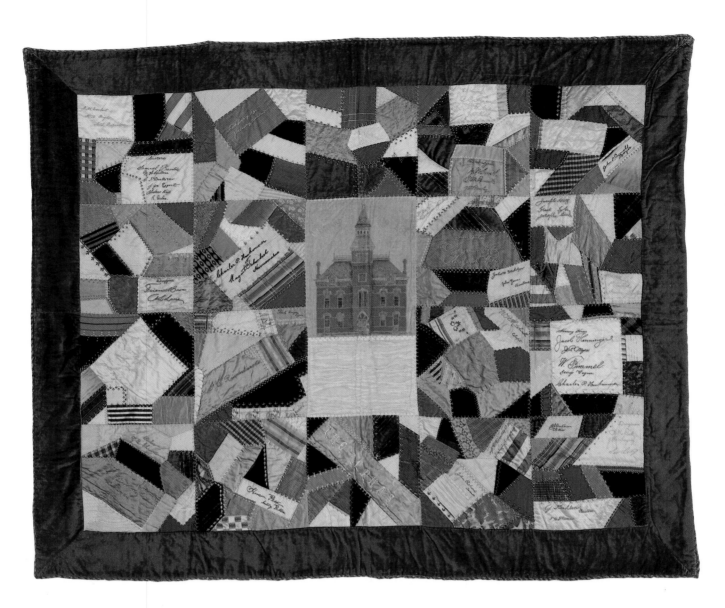

97, 97a. Monroeville Town Hall quilt, Monroeville, Ohio, 1888, 48″ × 60″. This quilt originated as a charity fund raiser for a group of Monroeville women. They charged town merchants—barbers, harnessmakers, farmers, grain dealers, and printers—for the privilege of signing their names to the quilt, which was to be displayed at the county fair. The center quilt block shows a painted representation of the town hall, probably done with stencils, known as *theorems,* which were cut from tracings of engravings or photographs. Photograph by John Glascock. (Collection of Firelands Historical Society Museum)

98. Winter carnival quilt, by Elizabeth Waller, Chicago, Illinois, 1886–1891, 72″ × 60″. Elizabeth Waller must have been entranced by the sight of the Ice Palace at St. Paul's first winter carnival in 1886. She spent the next five years working on this crazy quilt, in which the Ice Palace was given a place of honor in the quilt's center. The palace is stuffed from behind to make it stand out from the block's background, and it is encrusted with beads of all kinds. Beads are also used on the background of the block to suggest twinkling stars and a crescent moon. (Mrs. Waller came to the United States from England, where fancywork was commonly enriched with beads.) In addition to the Ice Palace, Mrs. Waller fashioned a fabric White House on another quilt block. Large palatial buildings must have held a fascination for her: her granddaughter recalls three-dimensional castles made of satin and chenille, which filled the walls of her grandmother's home in Chicago. (Collection of Minnesota Historical Society Museum Collections)

99, 99a, 99b. Hardman medallion quilt, by Mrs. Edwin Hardman, New York City, last quarter of the nineteenth century, 82″ × 70″. It's hard for the Victorian house in this quilt's center to hold our interest completely because the surrounding scenes give it such keen competition for our attention. The Hardman medallion quilt can only loosely be considered a crazy quilt, but the few blocks of crazy patchwork on it provide the perfect excuse for including it in this book. (Collection of The Haggin Museum, Stockton, California)

Quilts Made for People

Like other types of quilts, crazy quilts were often made as gifts for people special to the quiltmaker or in memory of loved ones. Not only could a crazy quilt be made with fabric once worn by the person for whom the quilt was made (any quilt could boast this), but a crazy quilt could also bear symbols of the person: fa- vorite flowers, birth dates, outlines of their hands, ribbons from meetings attended, and so on. Quilts were made for public figures as well as friends and family members. Dozens of crazy quilts were made, for example, for the convalescing President Garfield after he was shot in 1881.

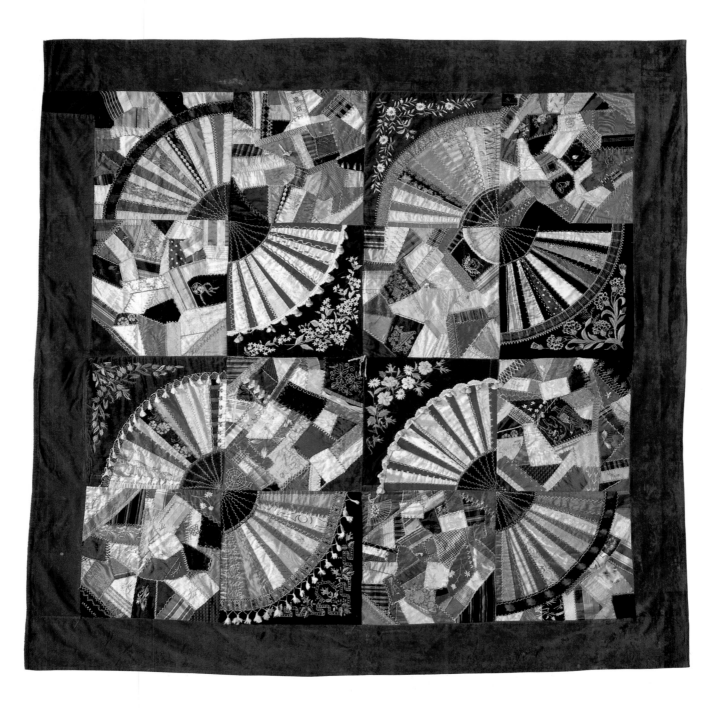

This quilt was made as a wedding gift for Maria Clementine Angeline Ronnebaum by her mother, Josephine Dobt Ronnebaum. Josephine was a widow who had been left with three children to raise; the youngest, a boy, was born a few months after her husband's death. The family lived with Josephine's mother-in-law, Anna Maria M. Ronnebaum Kinker, who helped her make a quilt for each of the three children as they were married. Maria Clementine was the middle child. She and her older sister, Mary, married men who were brothers.

Maria Clementine and her husband, George Kasselmann, had eight children, and their wedding crazy quilt took on a special function with the birth of each child. The children were all born at home, and when Maria Clementine was ready to receive visitors and show off the new baby, the quilt would be brought down from the attic and placed on the bed. Every spring, on a clear and windy day, the quilt was given an airing by being hung over the line in the backyard, where it became a great conversation piece among the neighbors who gathered to admire it.

101. George A. Kasselmann and his bride, Maria Clementine Angeline Ronnebaum, on their wedding day, April 24, 1894, in Cincinnati, Ohio. The bride wears a satin-and-lace two-piece wedding dress with an eighteen-inch waistline and an orange-blossom-wreathed veil. The wedding costume has been handed down in the family, along with the crazy quilt. (Courtesy of Barbara Kasselmann)

100, 100a. Crazy quilt with fan blocks made by Josephine Dobt Ronnebaum and her mother-in-law, Anna Maria M. Ronnebaum Kinker, Cincinnati, Ohio, 1894, 92″ × 88″. Photograph by John Kluesener. (Collection of Barbara Kasselmann)

102. Crazy quilt, Pennsylvania(?), 1887–1888, 80″ × 76″. Not only is this a snappy-looking quilt, but it contains a rebus, which you can find quite easily without being told where to look. Bells ring in the New Year on this quilt, and the quilt owners suggest that Sallie Fite might be a baby whose birth made her the New Year's gift. Small embroidered hands at the top of the quilt are marked "Sallie 12 Months" and "Sallie 6," probably standing for six months. Another hand bears the word *gift*. (Collection of Mary Strickler's Quilt/ Linda Reuther and Julie Silber)

103. Crazy quilt, embroidered, c. 1890, 84″ × 68″. This quilt bears cross-stitched religious sayings and exquisitely embroidered flowers. It's quite possible that the flowers were chosen for their symbolic meanings in order to strengthen the moralistic tone of the quilt. Here are some of the quilt's flowers and their "meanings" in flower language:

Daisy	Innocence, hope
Holly	Foresight
Lilac	Humility
Grapes	Charity
Violet	Faithfulness
Red rosebud	Purity and loveliness

The bottom of the quilt is inscribed, "Made for Frances Willard by her Mother, Mary T. H. Willard." Frances Willard was a leader in the Women's Christian Temperance Union. (Collection of Nancy Starr)

104. Crazy quilt, by Stella Timberlake May, Aspen, Colorado, 1901–1911, 59″ × 79″. The inscription "To C. H. Timberlake From Mama" in the center of the quilt suggests that it was made for Stella May's son. Whether or not it was, looking at the quilt is like turning the pages in an old album full of mementos. Stella May grew up in Ohio and moved to Colorado in the 1870s. She married Willette Charles Timberlake—referred to on the quilt as Willie, and by the initials *WCT*—who died in 1890, leaving her with two sons. The C. H. Timberlake that the quilt is inscribed to was her son Charles. Her other son was named Earl, and a small pocket near the bottom of the quilt holds a handkerchief and bears his name.

Five years after her first husband's death, Stella was remarried, this time to a railway fireman named John May. A faded red ribbon printed with the word *floor* was embroidered "J. I. May—7.4.94," the year before their marriage. The quilt also contains a ribbon from a fireman's muster: the Aspen Hose Team. Stella's sister Abbie also lived in Aspen, having married a professional gambler, a man who was killed in a gambling argument eight years after their marriage. Abbie is represented on the quilt by a butterfly sewn with gilt thread. This seems to be an appropriate symbol, for Abbie's husband took great pride in her looks and, while he was winning, bought her beautiful dresses and jewels (which reportedly were later sold to pay off debts). Some of the fancy fabrics in the quilt are said to have come from Abbie's dresses. Whether or not Stella's quilt was made for her son Charles, it was never passed down to him. Both Charles and his brother, Earl, died in their twenties, and Stella and her husband left Aspen. The quilt was eventually left to Stella's niece and namesake. Photograph courtesy Visual Arts Center, Aspen, Colorado. (Collection of Aspen Historical Society)

105, 105a, 105b. Crazy quilt, c. 1900, 70″ × 60″. Julie Silber, one of the owners of this quilt, says that it was made by a widow who took her mourning coat, opened it up at the seams, and made a mourning quilt with a central coffin shape to tell the story of her life with her husband. The quilt has pieces that may be from a wedding dress, embroidered flags, and a sailboat, as well as such symbols of love as red roses and paired hearts. There is also a pansy for remembrance, and the lilies and fallen leaves stand for death. The lines of embroidery, which are at times even and regular and at other times wildly erratic, seem to express the quiltmaker's changing moods.

Victorian mourning customs were established by the example set by Queen Victoria after the death of her husband and her mother in 1861. During the period of "deep mourning," lasting at least a year after a death, widows appeared in public only in black and with their faces veiled. After "deep mourning" came a period of "half-mourning," during which clothing of gray and, later, soft violet could be worn. (Collection of Mary Strickler's Quilt/ Linda Reuther and Julie Silber)

Six Quiltmakers

Many crazy quilts are not anonymous. We know who made them either because they were signed and dated, or because they were carefully passed down through generations in a family, along with the name and the history of the quiltmaker. The following six crazy quilts are a sample of such family treasures.

106, 106a–106c. *My Crazy Dream,* by M. M. Hernandred Ricard, Boston, 1877–Haverhill, Massachusetts, 1912, 65″ × 60″. Certainly this quilt is the epitome of all that a crazy quilt should be. The random patches form a kaleidoscopic swirl around the central schoolhouse scene, which is inhabited by such curious creatures as a giant peacock towering over an elephant. Fans, flowers, birds, butterflies, and a wonderful spider trapping a fly in its web appear as calm islands in the storm of detail and pattern. A picture of the quiltmaker, M. M. Hernandred Ricard, can be found on a quilt patch toward the bottom of the quilt, along with the notation "Boston, 1877–Haverhill, 1912" and the marvelous title: *My Crazy Dream.* Photograph by Bill House. (Collection of Emily E. Johnson)

107. Maria Wilson Beardsley (1858–1946), Hamilton, Ohio. (Courtesy of Dorothy Leighton and Isabel Beardsley)

108. Crazy quilt, by Maria Wilson Beardsley, Hamilton, Ohio, c. 1883, 80″ × 55″. Maria Beardsley's crazy quilt was made when she was twenty-five years old. Her daughter recalls that all of the fabric for the quilt came from old ties, vests, and dress scraps from family and friends. None was purchased. Mrs. Beardsley and her husband put the patches on the floor and tried out various combinations before deciding on the final arrangement. (Collection of Ohio Historical Society)

109. Crazy quilt, by Mary Schelly Millikin, Hamilton, Ohio, c. 1883, 92½" × 62½". Mary Schelly Millikin was born in the same year and in the same small Ohio town as Maria Wilson Beardsley. One can't help but think they must have known one another, and wonder if they were friends who possibly are reunited on adjacent pages of this book. The Millikin quilt is noteworthy for its exquisite velvet border painted with roses, morning glories, iris, black-eyed Susans, water lilies, and cattails. Photograph by John Kluesener. (Collection of Paul T. Millikin)

110. Mary Schelly Millikin (1858–1897), Hamilton, Ohio. (Courtesy Paul T. Millikin)

109a. Detail, water lilies and cattails. *Harper's Bazar*, January 24, 1883: "The most prolific plant in the modern flora is, perhaps, the *Typha latifolia*, or the swamp cattail. . . . it was rediscovered by fashion ten years ago, since which date it is estimated that seventy thousand specimens of the two varieties known as the embroidered and the painted thrive in the parlors of the United States alone."

111, 111a. Crazy quilt, by Elvina Harter (1839–1921) Pennsylvania, c. 1880–1904, 74″ × 72″. Elvina Harter was born in Nittany Valley, Pennsylvania, on December 4, 1839. By the time she made this quilt, Elvina Harter was a widow, living with her son and daughter-in-law in Lockhaven, Pennsylvania. Judging from the sprigs of flowers covering the lattice strips and extending into the blocks, the final embroidery was added after the entire quilt top was assembled.

The surface of the quilt is unusually rich because of the thousands of beads that are sewn into the design, making up flower petals and lines of embroidery. There is also an amusing use of a spider-and-web design around the border of the quilt. The beaded spider is shown four times on the quilt, each time crawling closer toward the center of its golden web. Elvina Harter's crazy quilt was finished some time in or before 1904, for it was shown at the St. Louis Exposition of that year and was awarded a third prize. The quilt is now owned by Elvina Harter's great-granddaughter. Photograph by Lance Ferraro. (Collection of Peggy Stouck Petrucci)

112. Elvina Harter (1839–1921). Photograph courtesy Peggy Stouck Petrucci.

113. Mittie Barrier designed this marvelous work of folk art (dated 1920, 80″ × 70″) when she was a young woman of twenty-six, living at home in Salisbury, North Carolina, the home she was to live in for all but twelve years of her life. She sewed the background patches of the quilt in her upstairs bedroom, using scraps left over from making coats and suits: "I would be working that winter on my quilt upstairs after I got up my lessons. My daddy was down stairs and if I would make the least little move he would hear me and say for me to go on to bed."[85]

She drew the wonderful flowers, birds, horses, rabbits, and other animals on paper, then embroidered on top of the paper, following her own patterns and pulling out the paper when the embroidery was done. The quilt has survived years of use, and it often served to keep her children entertained inside the house while she went outdoors to milk cows. Mittie Barrier gave the quilt to her daughter, but after her daughter's death, Mittie embroidered the quilt with an inscription that reads: "Jan. 17, 1973, To Cathy, from Grand Mother Mittie," and gave the quilt to her granddaughter. (Collection of Cathy Shoe)

113a. Detail, squirrels gathering acorns. "I couldn't get any gray thread anywhere. I took one of daddy's old socks and ravelled it up to make the squirrel."—Mittie Barrier

114. Mittie Belle Agner Barrier (1894–1977), Salisbury, North Carolina. (Courtesy of Cathy Shoe)

113b. Detail, alligators stalking ducks. "We had these animals around here, goats, cows, chickens and horses. . . . But not the alligators."—Mittie Barrier

113c. Detail, birds with eggs in a nest. Notice how long, straight stitches of brown thread were used to construct the nest. This block is one of three scenes on the quilt showing nesting birds.

113d. Detail, goat surrounded by geese and chickens. Notice how the angry goose in the center of the flock adds life to the whole block.

113e. Detail, rabbits and chickens. This is one of two egg-and-rabbit blocks in the quilt. The combination of rabbits, baby chicks, and colored eggs in a basket turns this into an Easter scene.

113f. Detail, chickens and rooster. These plump barnyard fowl almost seem to be molded out of thread. The rooster is a beautiful example of an original use of long and short satin stitches that are woven in and out, defining breast and wings.

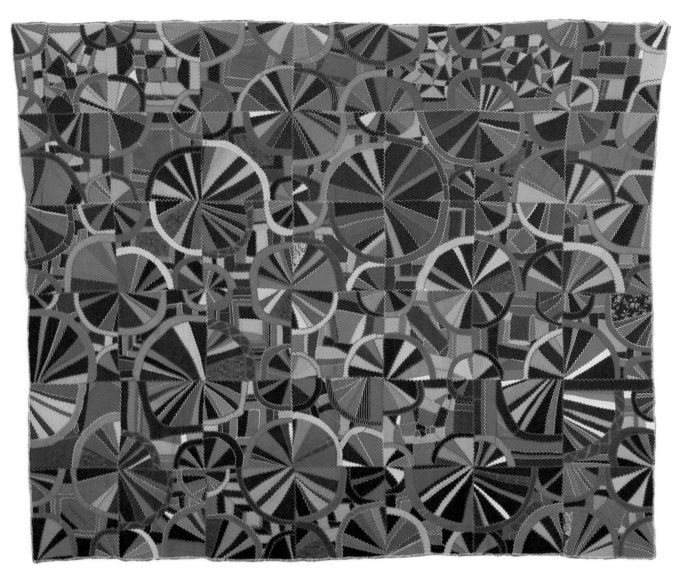

115. Crazy quilt, by Susan Nokes McCord, McCordsville, Indiana, c. 1880–1900, 80″ × 66″. Susan McCord was born in Ohio but lived most of her life as a farm wife in Indiana. She is one of those rare quiltmakers from whom a large known body of work remains. Ten of her quilts are now in the Henry Ford Museum, and three others are still owned by the family. Of the quilts in the Ford Museum, three are crazy quilts. This is perhaps the most striking of the three. The swirling "wheels" are formed by fan designs on each block, with four fans joining visually to make a wheel. The wheel "rims" form irregular serpentine lines that give the quilt a sense of movement and life. (Collection of Greenfield Village and Henry Ford Museum)

116. Susan Nokes McCord (1829–1909) McCordsville, Indiana. (Courtesy Mildred McKesson)

Country Crazy Quilts

Women fashioned crazy patchwork out of whatever fabrics they had. If they couldn't get silk plushes, satins, and velvets, they often used cotton and wool. Whatever the materials, making fancywork gave women an excuse to sit down and rest for a while, and to work on a project on which they could see daily progress being made, unlike most housework, which is done day in and day out. It also involved women crea-tively, which must have lifted their spirits momen-tarily. As one woman wrote, "I think it is a pleasant va-riety after the coarser work and unending array of plain sewing which is always confronting the house-keeper, to take up the soft materials whose bright colors refresh the eyes, and form them into tasteful or-naments for the home."[86]

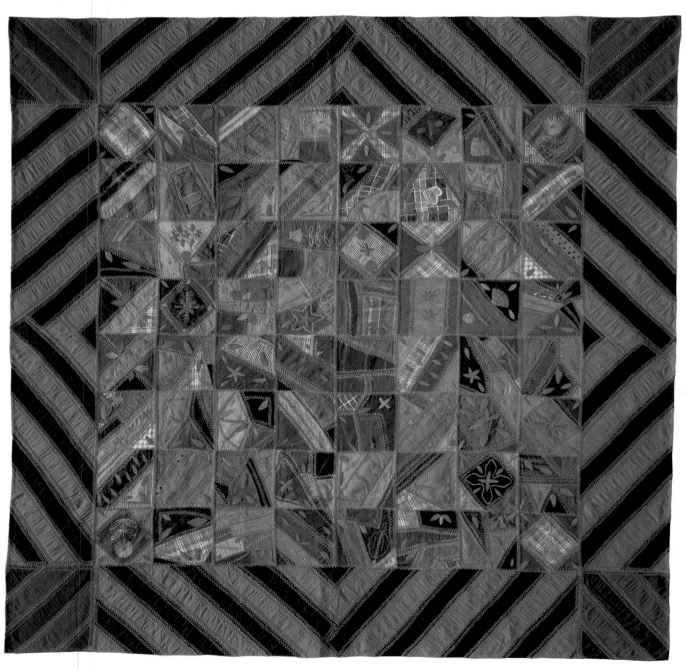

117, 117a. Crazy quilt, wool, Pennsylvania, c. 1890, 76" × 76". Feather stitching in red and blue wool outlines the patches and the border stripes, giving the whole quilt a purple glow. Notice the use of checked and plaid fabric which is somewhat unusual in a crazy quilt. Photograph by John Kluesener. (Collection of Sandra Mitchell)

118. Crazy quilt, wool and cotton, Pickens County, Alabama, c. 1900, 75″ × 65″. This rough country crazy quilt is softened by hearts and flowers and by the wistful inscription, "Think of Me." Photograph by George Flemming. (Collection of Helen and Robert Cargo)

119. Crazy quilt, wools, cotton, and silk, c. 1880–1910, 66¾″ × 75¾″. The original flower designs on this quilt are tufted so that they stand out from the quilt surface like rows of chenille. Cattails and crosses are done in the same heavy yarn. The patchwork is crudely done, but both the delicate and the heavier repeating primitive flower forms give the quilt a naïve folk art quality. (Collection of Helen L. Allen Textile Collection, The University of Wisconsin–Madison)

120. Crazy quilt with hearts, wool, Amish, Lancaster County, Pennsylvania, c. 1900, 66″ × 72″. As far as is known, this is a unique example of an Amish quilt incorporating the heart motif. (Kelter-Malcé Antiques, New York City)

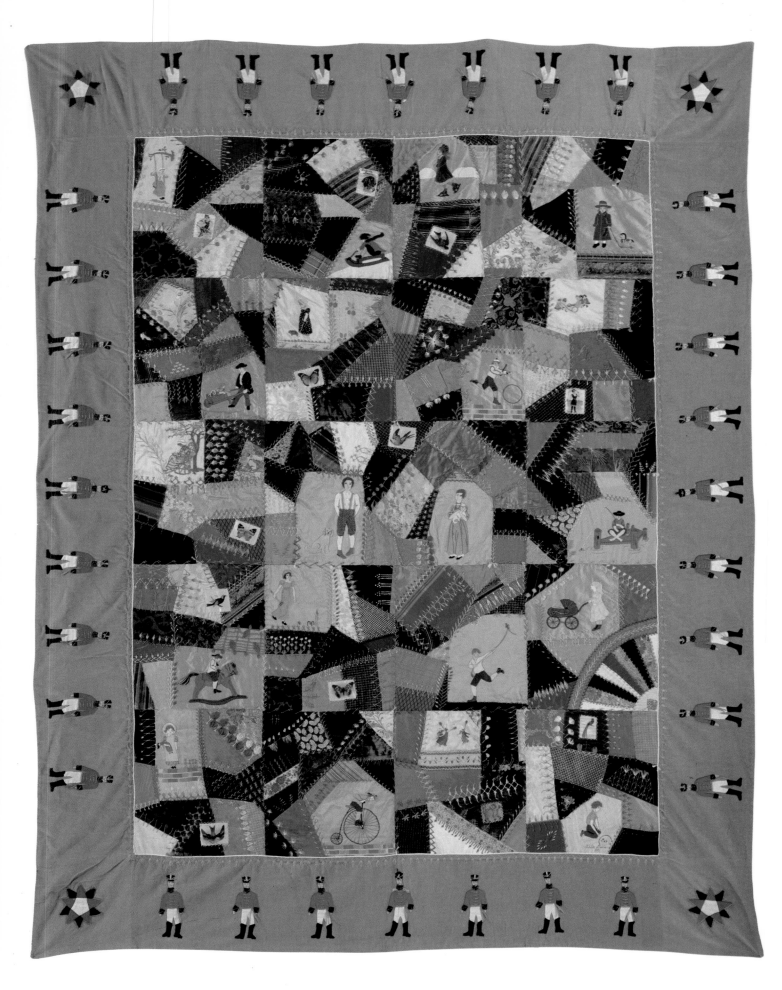

Contemporary Influences

Interest in crazy patchwork peaked in the 1880s and 1890s and has been at a low point since about 1910. Recently, however, some quiltmakers and artists have based their designs on the random patterning inherent in the crazy quilt, creating original designs for the present that also serve to reawaken interest in crazy quilts of the past.

121, 121a–121d. *Toy Soldier Crazy Quilt,* by Addie Mangoian Davis, Friendship, Indiana, 1980–1981, 99″ × 77″. Addie Davis writes of her quilts:

> . . . what started out as a hobby to fight boredom became a compulsion . . . to create and leave something beautiful when I depart this life as evidence that I have passed this way. . . . I love the Crazy Quilts so very much and I'm puzzled by the attitude of quilt experts who don't accord them the same consideration they do pieced and appliquéd quilts. If they [the experts] would only try and make one, their attitude about Crazy Quilts would change, I'm sure, and Crazy Quilts would get the respect as an art form I think they rightly deserve.[87]

Addie designed this quilt to depict children from the 1800s. Some of the designs are Kate Greenaway figures, but many others are original designs based on children from the small Indiana town (population 82) in which she lives. The girl near the center of the quilt, holding a cat in her arms, is taken from an old folk painting. Addie used small beads on the high-button shoes and even knitted a tiny wool cap, socks, and scarf to dress the red-coated boy with a sled near the top of the quilt. Of the delicate embroidery edging the quilt patches she writes, "I made the embroidery as fancy as I could, copying from photographs of old Crazy Quilt throws and recreating and figuring out 'how' with the use of a magnifying glass." To complete the quilt, she appliquéd thirty-two tin soldiers along the border. She used tiny brass beads for the buttons of their double-breasted coats, white linen for their pants, and black polished cotton to simulate leather boots and hats. The center soldier in each row was given golden epaulets, a black hat feather, and a bright blue sash—suitable finery for an officer. Photograph courtesy Thos. K. Woodard, American Antiques & Quilts, New York.

122, 122a. *Fancy Victorian Throw*, by Addie Mangoian Davis, Friendship, Indiana, 1982, 59″ × 73″. Designs on this quilt include "Jimmy," the red-coated fireman from the weathervane atop the Madison, Indiana, fire station, and a fan with queens' faces made from silk cigarette premiums. The same girl holding a cat that appeared on the *Toy Soldier* quilt shows up again, this time standing on a cigarette-premium Oriental rug. Next to her is Addie Davis's neighbor, Danny. Addie writes about that appliquéd patch:

> Funny thing about the boy, his hat didn't turn out quite the way I wanted but I used it anyway. Hat is unique and funny. About a month later, Danny showed up with an identical hat. I don't know where he found the hat or why he got it because I had not mentioned to him that he was included on the throw nor did I show him the finished appliqué of the boy.

Many of the figures done in outline stitch along the black border are taken from Kate Greenaway designs or from weathervanes. At the top left-hand corner is a good-luck horseshoe. Addie persuaded a local blacksmith to lend her his sample board showing different types and sizes of horseshoes so that she could choose one for tracing a pattern. Photograph courtesy Thos. K. Woodard, American Antiques & Quilts, New York.

123. *A Crazy Crib Quilt for Babies Grand,* by Catherine Ryan, Maryland, 1979–1980, mixed media: pieced and quilted fabric, porcelain figures, 66″ × 41″ × 3″. Catherine Ryan thought of the music of her favorite composers and used crazy patchwork strips to show how the music would look if she could see it as well as hear it. Each composer is shown as a baby, beneath his musical strip. The busts are amusing reminders of the clay figures given as rewards to good piano students. (Collection of the artist)

123a. Detail, *A Crazy Crib Quilt for Babies Grand,* by Catherine Ryan.

124. *Ragtime Disaster*, by Gayle Fraas and Duncan Slade, Maine, 1983, pima cotton painted with Procion dyes, machine- and hand-quilted, 24″ × 24″. In this slightly surrealistic scene, scraps of cloth flutter from a clear night sky into a mysteriously ambiguous space occupied by two crazy-quilted beds. Courtesy the artists.

125. *Remembering Chicken Little,* by Jan Myers, Minnesota, 1981, Procion-dyed cotton, machine-pieced and -quilted, 47″ × 40″. If you remember the story of Chicken Little, you'll recall his cry of "The sky is falling." This quilt has blocks arranged so that tiny snips of color seem, indeed, to be falling from the sky. Courtesy the artist. (Collection of Gordon and Ruth Donhouse, St. Paul, Minnesota)

126. *Crazy Quilt Teapot,* by Richard Marquis, California, 1978–1979, colored glass mosaic, fused and blown, H. 6″.

127. *The Three Fiancés,* by Robin Lehrer Roi, New York City, 1980, watercolor, 50″ × 60″. This watercolor is a concrete example of the effect of crazy patchwork on a work of contemporary art. The artist has painted pattern upon pattern, composing the painting's center section in the same random manner in which one would arrange patches in a crazy quilt. Courtesy the artist. (Collection of Mr. and Mrs. Robert Schneebeck, Cincinnati, Ohio)

128. Trousseau robe, 1880–1900 (back view with fronts shown open at sides). Courtesy Gracie Larsen. (Collection of Gheen Abbott III, on loan to The Lace Museum, Mountain View, California)

Appendix

Care of Victorian Silk Quilts and Slumberthrows

DIVISION OF TEXTILES, THE NATIONAL MUSEUM OF AMERICAN HISTORY, SMITHSONIAN INSTITUTION

Many elaborately embroidered and painted parlor throws and bedcovers of velvet, satin, and other fancy silks that were so popular in the late Victorian era have been treasured and preserved. Because a wide variety of fabrics, embroidery yarns, and other decorative materials were used in making them, their preservation presents special problems.

Many of the silk fabrics used in crazy quilts are weighted with mineral salts and other substances. This means the fabrics have been coated with, or have actually absorbed these substances to give them more weight and a stiffer texture. Unfortunately, weighting substances also speeds up the fabric's deterioration.

Silk is extremely susceptible to light damage which can be seen in brittleness, splits, and the eventual powdering of the yarns. Sometimes, even though a piece of silk may appear in perfect condition, it can be extremely fragile. Unfortunately, we know of no way to stop this deterioration, or reverse it. We can, however, slow it down by keeping the textile out of bright household lighting, and *especially fluorescent light and sunlight.* If a quilt is to be displayed, it should be protected by keeping the room's draperies drawn, the light level low, and the lighting fixtures at a distance from the quilt.

Dust and dirt can do a great deal of harm to silk quilts, as can wet-cleaning and dry-cleaning. Dust, and especially dirt, can actually cut fibers as they expand and contract with changes in temperature and humidity. If the dust or dirt present becomes wet, it could act as a dye and penetrate and stain the fabric. It can then become impossible to remove.

Dry-cleaning has a drying effect on textile fibers and puts a great deal of physical stress on the fabric. In addition, since very little research has been done on the long-range effects of dry-cleaning, it is not recommended for an antique textile whose long-term preservation is at stake.

Wet-cleaning can be damaging to silk quilts because quite often the dyes and paints used are not fast to water, and will run and redeposit on adjoining sections. The salts, and other substances used in weighting the fabric, are not waterfast either, and little research has been done on the long-range effects of removing these salts. These factors, combined with the many layers of fabric present, make the wet-cleaning of a silk quilt so complex that it is not recommended.

The only completely safe method of cleaning that is possible on a silk quilt is vacuuming. This will remove a great deal of airborne dust and dirt that can cut and stain the fibers. To vacuum a quilt, cover it with a piece of screening, preferably fiberglass-coated window screening, and run a very low-power hand vacuum over the surface. If a quilt is extremely fragile, it may be necessary to hold the cleaner a half-inch or more above the surface of the quilt. The vacuum cleaner will draw out the dust and dirt, while the screen will prevent the fabric from being sucked upward and damaged. Some quilts, however, may be too fragile to withstand even this type of cleaning.

Frayed, split, and torn patches may be covered with fine silk organza or crepeline. (Crepeline is a fabric made especially for textile conservation work. Silk organza is not as sheer as crepeline, but could be found easily in most fabric stores.) Using a very fine needle and silk thread or the warp yarn from the silk organza, attach the fabric to the quilt over the damaged patch. Use as few stitches as possible, making them no less than a quarter of an inch long, remembering that each time a needle is passed through the quilt a permanent hole is made. It is best to use seams as attachment points, as they are usually the strongest parts in the quilt.

A silk quilt should be stored in a clean, dry, dark area. It should have no direct contact with wood, ordinary paper, or paper products. Depending upon its construction and condition, a silk quilt may be folded and placed in a drawer lined with acid-free buffered paper or smooth, washed, unbleached, undyed muslin. The fold should be padded with muslin or buffered paper to avoid permanent creasing and splitting. The folds should be changed several times a year to minimize further damage. Nothing heavy should be placed on top of the quilt. Another piece of buffered paper or muslin should be used to cover the quilt to protect it from the elements. Never seal silk quilts, or any other antique textile in a plastic bag as there is a danger of moisture condensation, as well as acid damage from the fumes given off by some types of plastic. If some type of plastic cover is necessary to prevent water damage cover the textile completely with polypropylene plastic, leaving a small area unsealed to assure proper air circulation.

NOTE: Remember that your object may provide evidence of value to future scholars. You are strongly recommended to show it to a professional conservator and seek his advice rather than treat it yourself. The Smithsonian Institution disclaims responsibility for any possible ill-effects of applying these recommendations to an object.

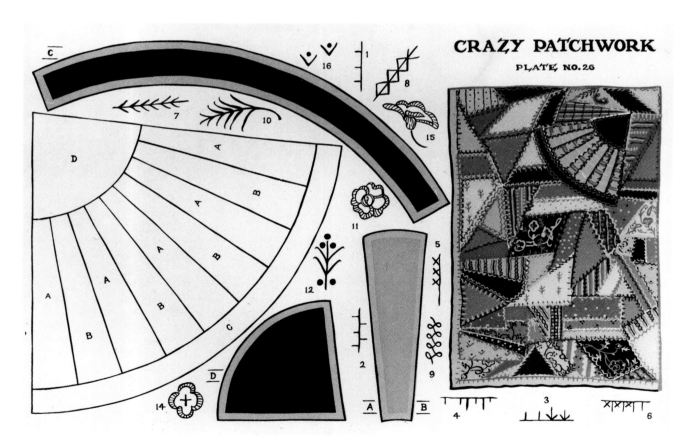

129. This fan pattern for use in crazy patchwork is one of thirty quilt designs (all based on actual quilts) reproduced in a portfolio titled "Quilts: Pieced and Appliquéd." This portfolio was a Works Projects Administration project of about 1935 for District Two in Pennsylvania.

Notes

1. *Webster's New World Dictionary of the American Language,* College Edition, 1960 ed., s.v. *crazy quilt.*

2. Ruth E. Finley, *Old Patchwork Quilts and the Women Who Made Them* (Philadelphia: J. B. Lippincott, 1929; reprint ed., n.p.: Charles T. Branford Company, 1980), 32.

3. Sally Garoutte, "The Scrappy Mother," *Quilters' Journal* (Summer 1978), 11–12.

4. *Godey's Lady's Book* (May 1883), 463.

5. *The Decorator and Furnisher* (January 1884), 148.

6. *The Cultivator and Country Gentlemen* (November 28, 1878), 766. This reference was first noted by Carol Crabb. The March 28, 1878, issue also discussed the crazy cushion (p. 206).

7. M. Hemingway & Sons' Silk Co., *A Lady's Book on Art Embroidery in Silk: with Engraved Patterns* (n.p.: M. Hemingway and Sons, n.d.), 25.

8. *Godey's* (May 1883), 462.

9. *Arthur's Home Magazine* (February 1885), 136.

10. *Harper's Bazar* (June 14, 1884), 382.

11. This connection between a crazing mill and the name *crazy quilt* was mentioned in a letter from Averil Colby to Sally Garoutte, October 1, 1978.

12. *Mosaic patchwork* is a term that is sometimes used for crazy quilts, and that is sometimes used for quilts made completely of hexagons.

13. *Harper's Bazar* (September 16, 1882), 583.

14. *Godey's* (October 1855), 381.

15. *Harper's Bazar* (September 16, 1882), 583.

16. *Ibid.* (June 3, 1882), 343.

17. *The Queen, The Lady's Newspaper* (London), January 26, 1884, 94.

18. Frank Norton, ed., *Frank Leslie's Illustrated Historical Register of the Centennial Exposition* (New York: Frank Leslie's Publishing House, 1877), 251.

19. The pattern of flower blossoms seen against a cracked-ice or spiderweb background may have been introduced to American women by English designers from the Royal School of Art Needlework in London. One of their designs of this type appeared in the January 15, 1881, *Harper's Bazar* as a bellows cover decorated with spiders' webs and trailing vines. The July 23, 1881, issue of *Harper's Bazar* printed an embroidery design of sunflower blossoms against cracked ice, by the American needlework designer Candace Wheeler. The September 19, 1885, *Harper's Bazar* showed a Royal School spiderweb and blossom design for use on music cases. In an editorial on Japanese art, *Peterson's Magazine* (July 1883 [84]) described Japanese design in a way that calls to mind the cracked-ice design: "The greater part of the space to be covered is broken up by patterns interlacing each other often with astonishing intricacy." This also is a good description of crazy-quilt random patching.

20. *Harper's Bazar* (December 18, 1880), 801.

21. *Ibid.* (July 25, 1885), 475.

22. James D. McCabe, *The Illustrated History of the Centennial Exhibition* (Philadelphia: The National Publishing Co., n.d. [around 1876–1877]), 27.

23. As early as August of 1855, *Godey's* printed an article on the women of Japan. The October 1860 issue of *Godey's*

discussed why Japanese women were educated; the answer: so that the wife might entertain her husband in his hours of leisure.

24. *Harper's Bazar* (June 11, 1881), 383.

25. *Godey's* (August 1880), 203.

26. *Peterson's Magazine* (July 1883), 82.

27. John Ruskin, of Queen's Gardens, Section 68, in *Works*, E. T. Cook and A. D. O. Wedderburn, eds., London, 1902-1912, Vol. 18, 122; quoted in Anthea Callen, *Women Artists of the Arts and Crafts Movement: 1870-1914* (New York: Pantheon Books, 1978), 20.

28. *The Ohio Farmer* (January 27, 1883), 66.

29. Mrs. C. S. Jones and Henry Williams, *Beautiful Homes: How to Make Them* (New York: Henry S. Allen, 1885), 7.

30. Jones and Williams, *Beautiful Homes*, 307.

31. *Dorcas Magazine* (October 1884), 263.

32. *Harper's Bazar* (August 2, 1879), 486.

33. *Godey's* (February 1864), 198.

34. *Arthur's Home Magazine* (January 1883), 57.

35. *Peterson's* (November 1882), 402. Fancywork is equated with patent medicine in the short story "Bessie's Silk Patchwork." The heroine, Bessie, says of fancywork, "It tranquilizes all my system." *The Cultivator & Country Gentleman* (August 24, 1882), 672.

36. *Dorcas Magazine* (June 1884), 174.

37. *The Ohio Farmer* (June 23, 1883), 458.

38. *Ibid.* (June 3, 1882), 382.

39. *Ibid.* (July 14, 1883), 80.

40. *The Decorator and Furnisher* (May 1883), 68.

41. "Patchwork," *Harper's Bazar* (September 16, 1882), 583.

42. *Peterson's* (August 1884), 184.

43. "The Career of a Crazy Quilt," *Godey's* (July 1884), 78. This story also refers to muslin fabric sold as foundation backing for crazy patchwork. The fabric was prestamped to show where patchwork pieces should be placed in the making of the patchwork block.

44. *Ladies' Home Journal* (March 1884), 6.

45. "Bentley's Catalogue of Novelties in Art Needlework, Stamping Patterns, Lacework &c.: 1884-1885," collection Missouri Historical Society Library (St. Louis) n.p.

46. *Ibid.* Although Shiela Betterton's book *Quilts and Coverlets from the American Museum in Britain* mentions a crazy-patchwork kit advertised in *Godey's* in 1855, a search of *Godey's* did not turn up that advertisement. Perhaps a typographical error turned 1885 (a date when one would expect to see kit advertisements) to 1855 in the book.

47. *Harper's Bazar* (April 26, 1884), 270.

48. *Comfort Mazagine* (January 1935), unpaged.

49. *The Ohio Farmer* (December 5, 1885), 364.

50. *Ladies' Home Journal* (August 1886), 13.

51. *Ibid.* (June 1885), 6.

52. F. G. Quinton, *The Ohio Farmer* (September 26, 1885), 206.

53. The Royal School of Art Needlework was founded in 1872. Its main goals were to establish needlework as a profession for gentlewomen needing employment, and to revive embroidery as an art form. The school staged a very influential display of needlework at the Centennial Exposition and was in large part responsible for the rebirth of interest in embroidery in America.

54. "Crazy Patchwork: All the New Fancy Stitches Illustrated; and Plain Instructions for Making the Patchwork" (Philadelphia: Strawbridge and Clothier, 1884), unpaged.

55. *The Ohio Farmer* (November 15, 1884), 318.

56. *Arthur's Home Magazine* (October 1884), 597.

57. *The Ohio Farmer* (July 19, 1884), 46.

58. *Harper's Bazar*, (May 10, 1884), 303.

59. *Dorcas Magazine* (September 1884), 253.

60. *Godey's* (February 1881), 178.

61. *The Queen, The Lady's Newspaper* (London), January 26, 1884, 94.

62. B. C. Saward, "Fashionable Embroidery," *Girls' Own Paper* (London), October 2, 1886, 11.

63. *The Ohio Farmer* (January 20, 1883), 46.

64. *Ibid.* (April 12, 1884), 266.

65. *The Ladies World* (June 1890), 7.

66. *The Ohio Farmer* (April 12, 1884), 266.

67. *Ibid.* (September 29, 1883), 206. Since the word *chow-chow* has sprung up twice, I feel that it needs a definition in case anyone, besides the author, needs one. Chow-chow is a relish made of chopped pickles in a highly seasoned mustard sauce.

68. *The Ohio Farmer* (March 3, 1883), 162.

69. *Ibid.* (March 24, 1883), 222.

70. *Harper's Bazar* (September 13, 1884), 578.

71. *Arthur's Home Magazine* (July 1884), 424.

72. *Ladies' Home Journal* (October 1894), 19.

73. *Harper's Bazar* (January 28, 1882), 55.

74. *Ibid.* (January 21, 1882), 40.

75. *Ibid.* (September 16, 1882), 579.

76. *Godey's* (July 1877), 93.

77. *The Ohio Farmer* (October 13, 1883), 238.

78. *Godey's* (September 1879), 286.

79. *Harper's Bazar* (October 23, 1880), 679.

80. *Ibid.* (September 27, 1884), 615.

81. *Godey's* (August 1878), 184.

82. *Harper's Bazar* (July 25, 1885), 475.

83. *Ibid.* (December 17, 1881 [811]) satirized the idea of a language of flowers in a short essay titled "The Language of Umbrellas": "There is a language of umbrellas, as of flowers.

For instance, place your umbrella in a rack, and it will indicate that it is about to change owners. To open it quickly in the street means that somebody's eye is going to be put out; to shut it, that a hat or two is going to be knocked off. An umbrella carried over a woman, the man getting nothing but the drippings of the rain, signifies courtship; when the man has the umbrella, and the woman the drippings of the rain, it indicates marriage. . . ."

84. Hallie Riddle; Birmingham, Alabama, 1887, quoted in *Black Belt to Hill Country: Alabama Quilts from the Robert and Helen Cargo Collection* (Birmingham Museum of Art, 1982).

85. Mittie Barrier, quoted in an interview in the *Salisbury Sunday Post* (Salisbury, North Carolina), April 21, 1974, 1B.

86. *The Ohio Farmer*, (February 4, 1882), p. 82.

87. All quotations from Addie Mangoian Davis are from a letter to the author.

Detail from quilt by Maria Wilson Beardsley, c. 1883, illustrated on pages 92–93. (Collection of Ohio Historical Society)

130. "Tile" crazy crib quilt, 21⅝'' x 21¾''. This fine miniature has the same appliqué construction as figures 44 and 45. Note how the fans in the lower left and right corners have become a basket of flowers in the upper left corner and a red-silk parasol in the upper right. (America Hurrah Antiques, New York City)

Selected Bibliography

ALFORD, LADY MARIAN. *Needlework as Art.* London: Sampson Low, Marston, Searle, & Rivington, 1886.

ANDREWS, GAIL C. Essay in *Black Belt to Hill Country: Alabama Quilts from the Robert and Helen Cargo Collection.* Birmingham: Birmingham Museum of Art, 1982.

ASLIN, ELIZABETH. *The Aesthetic Movement: Prelude to Art Nouveau.* London: Ferndale Editions, 1969.

BACON, LENICE INGRAM. *American Patchwork Quilts.* New York: William Morrow & Company, 1973, 110–125.

BATH, VIRGINIA CHURCHILL. *Needlework in America: History, Designs and Techniques.* New York: The Viking Press, 1979.

Bentley's Catalogue of Novelties in Art Needlework, Stamping Patterns, Lacework &c.: 1884–1885. New York: Chas. E. Bentley, 1885. (Missouri Historical Society Library, St. Louis.)

BETTERTON, SHIELA. *Quilts and Coverlets from the American Museum in Britain.* Bath, England: The American Museum in England, 1978, 95–98.

BISHOP, ROBERT, and COBLENTZ, PATRICIA. *New Discoveries in American Quilts.* New York: Dutton Paperbacks, 1975, 114–117.

———. *The World of Antiques, Art, and Architecture in Victorian America.* New York: Dutton Paperbacks, 1979.

———, and Safford, Carleton L. *America's Quilts and Coverlets.* New York: Weathervane Books, 1974, 296–303.

———, Secord, William, and Weissman, Judith Reiter. *Quilts, Coverlets, Rugs and Samplers.* The Knopf Collectors' Guide to American Antiques. New York: Alfred A. Knopf, 1982, 193–202.

BOND, DOROTHY. *Crazy Quilt Stitches.* Cottage Grove, Ore.: Author, 34706 Row River Road, 1981.

BROOKLYN MUSEUM, THE. *The American Renaissance: 1876–1917.* Brooklyn, N.Y.: The Brooklyn Museum, 1979.

CALLEN, ANTHEA. *Women Artists of the Arts and Crafts Movement: 1870–1914.* New York: Pantheon Books, 1979.

CARLISLE, LILIAN BAKER. *Pieced Work and Appliqué Quilts at Shelburne Museum,* Museum Pamphlet Series, No. 2. Shelburne, Vt.: The Shelburne Museum, 1957, 32–33.

CAULFIELD, S[OPHIA] F[RANCES]A[NNE], and SAWARD, BLANCHE C. *The Dictionary of Needlework: An Encyclopaedia of Artistic, Plain and Fancy Needlework.* London: A. W. Cowan, 1882. Reprint. New York: Crown Publishers, 1977.

CHRISTOPHERSON, KATHRYN D. "19th Century Craze for Crazy Quilts." *Quilters' Journal* (Spring 1978), 9.

COLBY, AVERIL. *Patchwork.* Newton Centre, Mass.: Charles T. Branford Co., 1958.

COOK, CLARENCE. *The House Beautiful.* New York: Charles Scribner's Sons, 1881.

Crazy Patchwork: All the New Fancy Stitches Illustrated; and Plain Instructions for Making the Patchwork. Philadelphia: Strawbridge & Clothier, 1884.

DEGRAW, IMELDA G. *The Denver Art Museum: Quilts and Coverlets.* Denver: The Denver Art Museum, 1974, unpaged.

DEWHURST, C. KURT; MacDOWELL, BETTY; and McDOWELL, MARSHA. *Artists in Aprons: Folk Art by American Women.* New York: Dutton Paperbacks, 1979.

EASTLAKE, CHARLES L. *Hints on Household Taste.* London: Long-mans, Green, 1868.

FINLEY, RUTH. *Old Patchwork Quilts and the Women Who Made Them.* 1929. Reprint. N.p.: Charles T. Branford Company, 1980.

GAROUTTE, SALLY. "The Development of Crazy Quilts." *Quilters' Journal* (Fall 1978), 13–15.

———. "The Scrappy Mother." *Quilters' Journal* (Summer 1978), 11–12.

GIFFORD, M. K. "Crazy Patchwork in Eastern Design." *Needle-work.* London: Thomas Nelson and Sons, n.d., unpaged.

GOSTELOW, MARY. *A World of Embroidery.* New York: Charles Scribner's Sons, 1975.

GROSS, JOYCE. "Emma Bull Crazy Quilt." *Quilters' Journal* 4, no. 4 (Winter 1982), 10–11.

HADERS, PHYLLIS. *The Warner Collector's Guide to American Quilts.* New York: Warner Books, 1981, 224–231.

HARBESON, GEORGIANA BROWN. *American Needlework.* New York: Coward-McCann, 1938.

HELLER, BOBETTE F. "A Historical Documentary of Crazy Patchwork and Descriptive Annotation of Crazy Patch-work in the Related Art—Allen Textile Collection." Spe-cial problem completed in partial fulfillment of master's degree, University of Wisconsin–Madison, 1969.

HOLSTEIN, JONATHAN. *The Pieced Quilt: An American Design Tradition.* Greenwich, Conn.: New York Graphic Society, 1973.

HUNGERFORD, MARY C. "Work for Idle Hours." *The Decorator and Furnisher* (July 1884), 138–139.

JENSEN, ROBERT, and CONWAY, PATRICIA. *Ornamentalism.* New York: Clarkson N. Potter, 1982.

JOHNSON, DIANE CHALMERS. *American Art Nouveau.* New York: Harry N. Abrams, 1979.

JONES, MRS. C. S. and WILLIAMS, HENRY. *Beautiful Homes: How to Make Them.* New York: Henry S. Allen, 1885.

A Lady's Book on Art Embroidery in Silk: with Engraved Patterns. N.p.: M. Heminway & Sons' Silk Co., n.d.

LICHTEN, FRANCES. *Decorative Art of Victoria's Era.* New York: Charles Scribner's Sons, 1950.

MCCABE, JAMES D. *The Illustrated History of the Centennial Exhibi-tion.* Philadelphia: National Publishing Co., 1876. Reprint. 1975.

MORRIS, BARBARA J. *Victorian Embroidery.* London: Herbert Jen-kins, 1962.

Needle and Brush. N.p.: The Butterick Publishing Co., 1889.

Needlecraft: Artistic and Practical. New York: The Butterick Publishing Company, 1889, 187–194.

NORTON, FRANK H., ed. *Frank Leslie's Illustrated Historical Regis-ter of the Centennial Exposition.* New York: Frank Leslie's Publishing House, 1877.

ORLOFSKY, PATSY, and ORLOFSKY, MYRON. *Quilts in America.* New York: McGraw-Hill Book Co., 1974.

"Ornamental Stitches for Embroidery." Lynn, Mass.: T. E. Parker, 1885.

"Ornamental Stitches for Embroidery." Augusta, Me.: P.O. Vickery, 1898.

"Ornamental Stitches for Embroidery." Augusta, Me.: Com-fort, n.d. [1911 or earlier].

Queen, The Lady's Newspaper (London), March 22, 1884, 315; January 26, 1884, 94.

RANDEL, WILLIAM PEIRCE. *Centennial: American Life in 1876.* Phil-adelphia: Chilton Book Co., 1969.

SEWARD, B[LANCHE] C. "Fashionable Embroidery." *Girls' Own Paper* (London), October 2, 1886, 11.

SILVESTRO, CLEMENT, and FRANCO, BARBARA. *Masonic Symbols in American Decorative Arts.* Lexington, Mass.: The Museum of Our National Heritage, 1976.

SWINNEY, H. J. "The Reassuring Quality of Victorian Adorn-ment." Foreword to *A Scene of Adornment: Decoration in the Victorian Home.* Rochester, N.Y.: University of Rochester, 1975.

WBGU-TV. "Crazy Quilts." From the series *Quilting*, Bowl-ing Green, Ohio, 1980.

WELTER, BARBARA. "The Cult of True Womanhood: 1820–1860." In Michael Gordon, ed., *The American Family in Social-Historical Perspective.* New York: St. Martin's Press, 1978, 224–250.

WHEELER, CANDACE T. *The Development of Embroidery in America.* New York: Harper & Bros., 1921.

WHITFORD, FRANK. *Japanese Prints and Western Painters.* New York: The Macmillan Company, 1977.

WICHMANN, SIEGFRIED. *Japonisme: The Japanese Influence on West-ern Art in the 19th and 20th Centuries.* New York: Harmony Books, 1981.

Periodicals

Arthur's Home Magazine, 1883–1885.

The Decorator and Furnisher, 1882–1884.

The Delineator, 1883–1885.

Dorcas Magazine, 1884–1886. (This needlework magazine was published only for two years.)

Godey's Lady's Book, July 1854–1856, 1864–1865, 1867, 1870, 1876–1885.

Harper's Bazar, 1872–May 19, 1877; 1879–March 27, 1886.

Ladies' Home Journal, 1884–1886.

The Ohio Farmer, 1881–1885.

Peterson's Magazine, 1868, 1881–1884, 1886.

Poems and Stories about Crazy Quilts

BENBERRY, CUESTA. "Piecework, Crazy and Appliqué." Poem in *Rhymes of Ruth's Round Robin*, vols. 1, 2 (1964).

"Bessie's Silk Patchwork." Story in *The Cultivator and Country Gentleman* (August 24, 1882), 672.

"The Career of a Crazy Quilt." Story in *Godey's Lady's Book* (July 1884), 77–82.

CARROL, MADGE. "A Crazy Quilt." Story in *Arthur's Home Magazine* (October 1885), 606–608.

CHITTENDEN, L. E. "A Story of a Crazy Quilt." Story in *Peterson's* (December 1885), 516–518.

"The Crazy Quilt." Poem in *Good Housekeeping* (October 25, 1890), 310.

HANSCOM, ALICE E. "Crazy." Poem in *Dorcas Magazine* (May 1884), 132.

Detail from quilt by Maria Wilson Beardsley, c. 1883, illustrated on pages 92–93. (Collection of Ohio Historical Society)

Index